PIG

SHAKESPEARE'S MOTLEY

Will Sommers   *Kinge Henory[e]s Iester*

Austen[?] ...[?] by Piters Iohn ...[?] who ...[?] in Cornewall. Franc Delaram[?]

That seeing the ...[?] mee clad in strange attire,   This Horne I haue, be greene, Semper Iam

newe I am ...[?] my owne desire,   Which sport in tyme, will bid ...[?]

...[?] see the Charackters describ'd vpon mee   All with my Nature well agreeing too

...[?] that a King best will them in   As hath the Name, and Temp ...[?]

SHAKESPEARE'S MOTLEY

BY

LESLIE HOTSON

HASKELL HOUSE PUBLISHERS Lᴛᴅ.

Publishers of Scarce Scholarly Books

NEW YORK, N. Y. 10012

1971

First Published 1952

SKELL HOUSE PUBLISHERS Ltd.
Publishers of Scarce Scholarly Books
280 LAFAYETTE STREET
NEW YORK. N. Y. 10012

Library of Congress Catalog Card Number: 75-117592

Standard Book Number 8383-1025-7

Printed in the United States of America

TO THE MEMORY OF
EDWARD STEVENS BEACH

CONTENTS

vii

ILLUSTRATIONS

I. THE MYSTERY OF MOTLEY

'IT seems strange that anyone should bother about detective stories ... when there lies open ... the rediscovery of Shakespeare's text through the initial rediscovery of the life and speech of Elizabethan England.'

This remark is not quoted from a scholar magnifying his speciality. It is the reflection of a common reader, a journalist who has realized that treasures still lie before our eyes unperceived on Shakespeare's page. For if we pause to think of it, we all know that the obvious difficulties in reading Shakespeare are trifling. When for instance we find King Edward declaring that 'Warwick was a bug that feared us all,' we automatically suspend judgment until the glossary assures us that Edward did not take the redoubtable Warwick for a cowrin' beastie, but 'a *bugbear* that *terrified* us all.'

The real Shakespearean puzzles are the ones we fail to notice. For if we *think we know* what a particular expression means, we don't even begin to wonder about it. Yet if we once take the unusual step of questioning the apparently obvious, the consequences can be startling. Suppose, for example, we take a common Shakespearean term, and permit ourselves to suspect that the sense we have universally accepted for it may be not at all what Shakespeare meant by it. How is the point to be settled? At a loss for a referee, we should never expect such luck as to find one of the poet's own friends and associates ready to come forward with an unequivocal explanation: an explanation so natural and apparently inevitable, that one wonders why in the world it has not occurred to us without his help. Yet this is just what has happened in the curious case to which I now invite your interest.

In the familiar Elizabethan word *motley*, used to describe the costume of a fool or jester, I find an unsuspected mystery. Its solution proves to be provided, and with a happy appropriateness, by Shakespeare's fellow-actor Robert Armin: 'honest, gamesome Robin' Armin, who succeeded the famous clown Tarlton, and struck out an original comedy line for himself. Armin was a wit, a rimester, a pamphleteer, and a playwright. On the stage, he was the gifted comedian and singer who bade the rustic russet clowns go by, and turned his keen attention to the study of Elizabethan 'innocents' or 'naturals'—that is, congenital idiots or born fools. It was Armin for whom Shakespeare was inspired to write the parts of the 'motleys'—Touchstone, Feste, and Lear's Fool—which surpass anything in that kind before or since. If Robin Armin had not been at his elbow to interpret him on the stage, Shakespeare would certainly not have made us these particular priceless gifts, living monuments to the genius of a player.

But where, you will ask, can one find any mystery in Shakespeare's use of the simple word *motley*? You may well suppose that this is one word at any rate in which the modern world understands him correctly. We are moreover all substantially agreed on its meaning: dictionary-makers, scholars, critics, Shakespearean producers, historians of stage costume—what Shakespeare's Lafew would call 'all the learned and authentic fellows.'

For a definition of it, open the *Encyclopædia Britannica*. What do we find? '*Motley*, i.e. of many colours, a term particularly used of the parti-coloured dress of the professional "fool" of the middle and later ages.' Ask the august *Oxford English Dictionary*: 'Motley, 3. A particoloured dress which was the recognized attire of a professional fool or jester.' Turn up Francis Douce, who since 1807 has been the standard authority on the dressing of Elizabethan Fools: 'The costume of the domestic fool in Shakespeare's time was of two sorts. In the first of these the coat was motley or parti-coloured ... the breeches and hose close, and sometimes each leg of a different colour ... the other dress, ... which seems to have been more common in the time of Shakespeare, was the long petticoat. ... It was, like the first, of various colours.' [1]

Query Dr. Percy Simpson, writing on the costuming of Fools in *Shakespeare's England* (1916): 'The traditional dress was the "motley" or "patched" suit with alternations of red and yellow. ... Another dress for the Fool was the long coat, borrowed from the dress of the natural idiot ... "a long motley coat ..." ' Call in Sir Arthur Quiller-Couch: 'To pass ... to our own appreciation of motley, can we not see Touchstone's suit—scarlet, we will say, down one side, and green down the other— illustrating his own contrast of wit and conduct, in speech after speech?' (*Shakespeare's Workmanship*, 97). Question Miss Lucy Barton (*Historic Costume for the Stage*, 221): 'This person [the jester], of whom Touchstone and Feste are examples, had his own livery. It is supposed that this sometimes included a long-skirted jerkin or a gown like the "blue-coat" [of the boys of Christ's Hospital].

---

[1] 'On the Clowns and Fools of Shakespeare,' in his *Illustrations* (1807), 507, 510.

Just as often, however, the Elizabethan jester wore a short-skirted costume, its style preserved from the fourteenth century: "chaperon" or hood, "cote-hardie" or doublet, and hose, all in "motley" or parti-colour.' And Sir Edmund Chambers, consulted on the point (*Medieval Stage*, I. 384), while sounding a characteristic note of caution, yet seems to agree that Shakespeare's fools appeared in this medieval dress: 'the costume just described, the parti-coloured garments, the hood with its ears, bells and coxcomb, and the *marotte* [sceptre or bauble], is precisely that assigned by the custom of the stage to the fools who appeared as *dramatis personæ* in several of Shakespeare's plays. See ... Touchstone in Miss E. Fogarty's "costume edition" of *As You Like It* ... it is not improbable that the tradition of the stage rightly interprets the intention of Shakespeare, [whose] actual texts are not very decisive. The point that is most clear is that the fool [in Shakespeare] wears a "motley" or "patched" coat.'

To be sure, on listening closely to this chorus of consent, we notice one or two unsupported assumptions. For example, *patched* and *parti-coloured* are assumed to be synonymous with *motley*. It is however at least remarkable that Shakespeare never links *motley* with either of these adjectives. Above all, if *motley* indeed signified the familiar parti-coloured dress of the medieval fool, how are we to explain the strange fact that the term is *never found used in that sense before Shakespeare's time*? Very curious! Furthermore, what of the already-mentioned 'tradition' of the stage which puts Shakespeare's Fool into a medieval parti-coloured jerkin (not a *coat*), long tight parti-coloured hose, and medieval *chaperon* or hood? If

4

the Elizabethans indeed saw their contemporary Fool in a *hood*—a sartorial survival familiar to them in the monk's cowl, the citizen's livery hood as a member of a London Company, and the lawyer's and graduate's academic hoods—why do they almost invariably describe their Fools' headgear (the readily-doffed article, often adorned with a simulated 'cock's comb,' which Lear's Fool offers to Kent) not as a hood, but as a *cap?* We still speak of the fool's cap and bells, and of foolscap paper. What reason have we to imagine that Shakespearean stage fools should wear hoods?[1]

On inspection, this 'tradition' of the stage proves to be no more than a latter-day and radically misconceived upstart. We need but glance at a chronological series of theatrical-costume prints to realize that the Eighteenth Century knew nothing of this gaudy medieval dress; and that the use of it for Shakespeare's Fools is no more than a modern fancy which pushed itself in with the Nineteenth Century and its medievalizing notions bred by the Romantic revival. We may be very fond of this gay

---

[1] Cf. *Pasquils Fooles-cap*; 'Thou art the cap of all the fools alive' —*Timon of Athens*, 4.3.365; 'No fooles cap with a bable and a bell' —Armin, *Foole upon Foole*, sig. A3ᵛ; 'Both my capp and my cote he bestowed on me'—*Misogonus*, 1.3.36; 'put on my cap and my coat' —Greene, *Friar Bacon and Friar Bungay*, 1.1.32; 'Coxcombes . . . *Because* naturall Idiots and Fooles *have, and still doe accustome themselves to weare in their Cappes*, Cockes feathers *or a hat with a* necke and head of a cocke *on the top, and a bell thereon, &c. and thinke themselves finely fitted and proudly attired therewith.*'—Minsheu, *Guide into Tongues* (1625); 'Brimborions . . . *the knacks, jags, nifles, bawbles, wherewith fools caps &c. are garnished.*'—Cotgrave-Howell, *French Dictionary*; '*Gepolkereert Sot*, A Foole or a Sot that weares a Fooles Cap'—Hexham, *Dutch Dictionary* (1658). The solitary rule-proving exception I have found in Shakespeare's lifetime occurs in *Martins Months minde* (1589), sig. G2ᵛ: 'my eldest sonne shall have my best sute; as Coate, whood, Coxcombe, and bable.'

costume of antiquity, but the plain fact is that it can claim no ground of authority in Shakespeare whatever.

What Shakespeare *does* tell us in the text of his plays is that his Fools wore a long motley *coat* or *petticoat*: 'I am ambitious for a motley coat'; 'a long motley coat guarded with yellow'; 'I did impeticos [impetticoat] thy gratillity [gratuity].' [1] On looking into the subject of 'coats' and 'petticoats,' we learn, as we might have expected, that Elizabethan petticoats, 'side' or long coats, like a woman's 'coats' or skirts, were robes which reached at least to the ankle. Dekker's Simon Eyre genially nicknames his Lord Mayor's scarlet gown 'my red petticoat.'

Shakespeare, we find, is always both knowing and exact in questions of costume, as becomes a player. Had he meant to describe the fool's costume as a shorter upper garment, he would have called it doublet or jerkin. But he meant what he said: a long coat or petticoat. If therefore we are able to shed our clinging romantic preconceptions and attend to Shakespeare himself, we must—however reluctantly—discard the antiquarian fancy of medieval hood, jerkin, and tight full-length hose, all in parti-colour, and see his contemporary figure of folly as he saw it: robed in a long 'motley' coat or petticoat, and topped with a cap.

A *motley* coat. This word brings us again to our mystery, the solution of which may throw some very interesting light. We may as well face the crucial question at once without shuffling. Was this long fool's coat made up of sewn-together halves, quarters, or patches of various pieces in contrasting bright colours? If that is indeed

---

[1] *As You Like It*, 2.7.43; *Henry VIII*, Prologue; *Twelfth Night*, 2.3.28,

6

what *motley* meant to the Elizabethans, a passage in Tom Coryate's report (1611) of his travel in France would seem to offer him a perfect chance of using the word *motley* to avoid a long explanation: 'About two miles on this side of Montrel there was a Whitsuntide foole disguised like a foole, wearing a long coate, wherein there were many severall peeces of cloth of divers colours.' [1]

The fact that Coryate must circuitously describe such a segmented and parti-coloured garment, instead of simply calling it 'a motley coat,' should give us pause. In the light of this, the question becomes imperative: was the motley coat of Shakespeare's Fool 'piecéd of divers colours' like that of Coryate's French fool, as we have thought for a century and a half, or was it something quite different?

Who really knows the answer? As we stand at a nonplus, enter Robert Armin—incontestably the cardinal authority on Shakespeare's Fools in motley, the only begetter of Touchstone, Feste, and Lear's Fool—to unriddle the riddle. Like Feste, Armin wears not the foolish 'motley in his brain': he has demolished harder problems than this of ours. As he comes downstage, we may fancy the learned Fool Armin saluting us with an exordium borrowed out of a contemporary book of Abraham Fleming's, as modest as it is morosophical: 'What cannot learning attain? What cannot the key of knowledge open? What cannot the lamp of understanding lighten? What secrets cannot discretion detect? Finally, what cannot experience comprehend?' For Armin is an ingen-

---

[1] *Crudities*, 9. And the contemporary essayist Sir William Cornwallis would seemingly reject a similar opportunity: 'It is a counterfaite fashion to face our foreparts with the rich stuffe of worth, and inwardly to bee a peeced stuffe of divers colours of divers ragges.'— 'Of Keeping State,' *Essayes* (ed. D. C. Allen), 89.

ious author as well as a player, and hereupon he opens one
of his own books—*Foole upon Foole, or, Six Sortes of
Sottes* (1600). It is a sympathetic and high-spirited
account of a half-dozen distinguished 'naturals' (fools flat,
fat, lean, clean, merry, and very), some of whom he knew
personally, and from whose assorted fooleries he distils
doses of shrewd human wisdom. Like his predecessor
Dick Tarlton, who delighted the public by extemporary
doggerel on the stage, Robin Armin breaks readily into
rime for a description of his first modern exhibit, 'Jacke
Oates,[1] being a flat [or positive] foole naturall':

> *Motley his wearing, yellow or else greene,*
> *A collored coate on him was seldome seene . . .*

What is this? A yellow motley, or a green motley, says
Armin, was *not* a 'coloured' coat! Unequivocal testimony,
from the premier player of fools in motley, that the
motley material of the 'flat fool's' coat, though it was
either yellow or green, was *not* 'coloured' or patched like
the coat of the fool Coryate met in France. Armin's
antithesis between *motley* and *coloured* is express. And
after calling Jack Oates a 'foole in motley,' he goes on (in
the later edition of his book) to show that Oates wore the
long coat or petticoat, which of course covered his de-
formed knees:

> *Writh'd i'th knees, yet who sees*
> *Faults that hidden be? . . .*
> *In Motly cotes, goes Jacke Oates,*
> *Of whom I sing this song.*

---

[1] Jack was a contemporary, flourishing A.D. 1587. See 'for a
paynted canne for John Oites, Sir William Holles fuelle, iij^d.'—
H. M. C. Rutland MSS., iv. 391.

As though further to drive home the clear contrast between *motley* and *colours*, Armin returns to the subject in the lively foreword to his later edition of *Foole upon Foole*, now renamed *A Nest of Ninnies* (1608). Like many Elizabethan authors, he apprehends ill-natured criticism of his book, and tries to forestall it. This irresponsible self-willed criticism he personifies as 'Censure,' and suggests that a varicoloured costume would suit the carper's wayward notions: 'They say he [Censure] goes in collours, as one strangely affected,[1] and I goe in Motly making my own cloakebag ready.'

Beyond making it plain once more that the fool's motley is *not* colours, Armin here equates *motley* with *cloakbag*: implying that motley, besides being the *material* proper for fools' wear, was also the *cloth* of which large and commonly-used portmanteaux were made. We shall return to *cloakbag*; but for the present Armin's revelation sends us back to the *Oxford English Dictionary*, this time not for a definition of the adjective (as 'a motley colour'), but of the noun—the *cloth* called 'motley': '*Motley* B. sb. 1. A cloth of a mixed colour; a mixture. *Obs[olete]*.' This is strange indeed. If the *cloth* motley was a *mixture*, or *of a mixed colour*, how could a costume of motley be parti-coloured? But let us look further. The *Dictionary*

---

[1] Compare Spenser, *F.Q.* 3.12.10: '*Doubt*, who was yclad in a discolour'd [i.e. varicoloured] cote.' And two passages in Jonson: '[Opinion's] gaudie *colours*, piec'd, with many folds, Shew what uncertainties shee ever holds'—*Hymenaei*; '*Danger* . . . the little garment shee hath left her, of severall colours, to note her various disposition'—*King's entertainment, in Passing to his Coronation*. Nashe too: 'And hee is counted no Gentleman amongst them [the Romans] that goes not in blacke: they dresse theyr jesters and fooles only in fresh colours, and say variable garments doe argue unstaiednes and unconstancie of affections.'—*Works*, ed. McKerrow, ii. 281.

continues with a quotation from Withals' *Dictionarie* (1556): 'he that maketh motley, *polymitarius*.' To explain this Latin term, the lexicon gives '*Polymitus, embroidered or weaved with threads of divers colours.*' And the *Oxford English Dictionary* then adds the following significant quotation: '1617 Moryson *Itinerary* III. 170 [The King of Denmark's] chief Courtiers ... were all attired in an English cloth, which they call Kentish cloth, we call Motley, but much finer than that whereof we make cloakebags.'

From all this it is now evident that the 'motley' of Shakespeare's Fools, like a homespun or a tweed, was a *mixture*, or *cloth of a mixed colour*. It was the *threads*, and *not* segments of material, that were of divers colours; and they were dyed in the wool. Yellow motley, then, would be a *mixture* in which yellow was the prevailing shade; and green motley a *mixture* showing chiefly green. The mystery is solved. It now looks as simple and as obvious as Columbus's egg; yet the fool's *motley* has fooled us all for a century and a half. It has taken Shakespeare's own motley Fool, the player Robin Armin, to open our eyes.

To set us right, and help to root out our inveterate misapprehension, I now find two apt passages for illustration. First, in a circular letter of the Privy Council of 1584, corrected in Lord Treasurer Burghley's own hand, prescribing equipment for soldiers levied for service in Ireland, we read that the footmen are to be 'furnished with ... a convenient dublett and hose, and also a cassocke [or overcoat] *of motley or other sad* [dark] *green coulor* or russet.' And second, the household book of Lord North tells us that on April Fools' Day, 1577, this peer made a seasonable purchase for his 'Foole lackey' of five and a half yards 'of motley for hose and cote,' or enough for breeches and long coat.[1]

Our unfamiliarity with this coarse mingled cloth and its associations has effectively blinded our eyes to what we now realize must be a misprint in the text of *The Taming of the Shrew*. We recall that when Petruchio turns up for his wedding in rags most fantastically outrageous, his sway-backed valetudinarian nag is said to carry 'an old *mothy* saddle.' That this is a misprint for *motly* becomes evident when we read in Lord North's household book of two 'new Motley saddells,' and in Queen Elizabeth's 1575–76 Warrants for the Great Wardrobe (L.C. 5/35/33, 41) of 'bardall saddles'—cloth pads for colts and asses—'Covered with motley,' and of 'one Saddle covered with motley . . . for Will our Foole.' The same misprint occurs in the *Promptuarium Parvulorum*: 'Mothey [i.e. Motley] colours. *Mixtura* [mixture],' and twice in Florio's Italian–English dictionary (1611): '*Mescolato* . . . a medlie or mothie [i.e. motlie] cloth; *Mischia* . . . a medly or mothy [i.e. motly] cloth.' Petruchio's choice of a saddle with which to mortify Kate gains point when we recognize it as a 'motley' pad, the homely furniture of asses and colts, for the riding of fools.

Looking back at the Elizabethans across the centuries, it is not hard to understand how the error which takes *motley* as *parti-colour* gathered strength in a subsequent age when most people had never heard of the Elizabethan cloth of *mingled* colour known as 'motley.' Yet the memory of its *various-coloured threads* evidently somehow survived, and became confused with the gay, pied,

---

[1] P.R.O., S.P. 12/175/103; B.M. MS. Stowe 774 f. 36.

patched, or parti-coloured style of the extreme Four-
teenth-Century fashions pictured in old manuscripts, or
with the pied Scaramouche and Harlequin costumes
brought in from the Continent in the Eighteenth Century.
It now seems most probable that the adjective *motley*, 'of
a mixed colour,' derives from the noun *motley*, 'a cloth of
a mixed colour,' just as we have the adjective *scarlet* from
the sumptuous fabric called *scarlet*, because it was cus-
tomarily dyed a brilliant red with cochineal or 'grain.'

Many conjectures have been offered for the etymology
of the word *motley*, but none carries conviction. The
well-established personal surname Motley, however,
suggests possible derivation from a place-name. Our
universally-known *worsted* got its name from the Norfolk
village of Worstead, 'a colony of Flemish weavers having
settled here in the 12th Century.' It might pay us to look
into the history and activities of places named Motley,
Mutley, or Matley. Cheshire has a Matley (Mutlow,
Motlowe), and a Mutley lies adjacent to Plymouth.
There may well be others.

Although early examples of confusion between the
epithets *motley* and *parti-coloured* certainly occurred (I
have found some in Elizabethan dictionaries), the mistake
probably became finally entrenched in the Eighteenth
Century. By marshalling all the relevant editions of
English dictionaries, one might perhaps disentangle the
motley imbroglio. I cannot claim to have done this, and
can but cite a few scattered examples for illustration. Dr.
Johnson's *Dictionary* (1755) gives '*Motley*, mingled of
various colours' and illustrates with the 'motley fool'
passages from Shakespeare. This looks as though Johnson certainly took the word to mean 'mixture' rather than

'parti-colour,' and that he had not departed from the Elizabethan sense. As late as 1782 N. Bailey's *Etymological Dictionary* (24th ed.) also clearly clings to it: '*Motley*, ... mixed, as a Motley Colour.' But meanwhile D. Fenning, in his *Royal English Dictionary* (4th ed. 1771), has gone over to the quite different modern sense: '*Motley* ... of various colours ... *Harlequin*, a person dressed in a motley-coloured jacket and trowsers ... *Scaramouch* ... A buffoon in a motley dress.'

Wherever it began, the modern misunderstanding of what Shakespeare meant by *motley* was strongly rooted by the time of Francis Douce, whose 'Dissertation on the dressing of theatrical clowns and fools in Shakespeare's time' (1807, quoted above) has wielded great influence ever since. But we must remember that Douce had evidently not seen Armin's extremely rare book, which would probably have set him right. He has therefore an excuse which J. P. Collier—who reprinted the *Nest of Ninnies* in 1842—and we latter-day students cannot offer. What is now at length clear beyond peradventure is that by 'motley' for a fool Shakespeare never means a pied or parti-coloured garment, but always one made of the coarse material of mixed colour, just as Armin does.

As to the *shape* of the motley worn by Shakespeare's fools, which we have already touched upon, Douce was misled, by his studies of illuminations, Fifteenth-Century drawings, and Continental illustrations which showed old styles, into imagining that *one* of the Elizabethan fool's costumes comprised the medieval hood, jerkin, and long tight hose, all in parti-colour, which it certainly did not. We must not however forget that he correctly insisted that *the form of the prevailing dress for the fool in Shake-*

speare's time was the idiot's petticoat. Thus he was partly right, which is more than can be said for some of his followers. In his own annotated copy of his book (Bodley MS. Douce Add. i. 87) Douce is unequivocal in controverting the eminent Shakespeareans George Steevens and Joseph Ritson on this point:

> 'Mr. Steevens has observed that "petticoats were not *always* a part of the dress of fools, though they were of idiots;" and on this assertion, coupled with another by Dr. Johnson, "fools were kept in long coats to which the allusion [*I did impeticos thy gratility*] is made," Mr. Ritson maintains that "it is a very gross mistake to imagine that this character [Feste] was habited like an *idiot.*" Now it is very certain, that although the idiot fools were generally dressed in petticoats, the allowed fool was generally habited in like manner.'

Yet, neglecting both Shakespeare's clear references to *cap* and *coat*, and Douce's sound emphasis on the petticoat, modern scholars and stage producers have clung to a Nineteenth-Century anachronistic picture of the Elizabethan fool in a medieval costume for which there is not a particle of authority in Shakespeare. If we ask, what difference does it make? the answer is that our innocent misconception will be seen to have blinded us to the true sense and connotation of several very significant passages in the plays.

To set about depriving the modern Shakespeare enthusiast of his time-honoured whimsical picture of the antique parti-coloured Fool is no light matter. Yet in what follows I trust he will find himself indemnified for the loss by a truer perception of Shakespeare's art. Certainly the actor, the leading partner in the latter-day

Shakespearean enterprise, will shed few tears over the loss of medieval hood and tights in assorted violent tints. Instinctively he *knows* that such a masquerade-dress is out of key with Shakespeare. It is pantomime stuff, and discourages his efforts to realize a subtle Elizabethan comic. The tricksy carnival disguise, with loud colours announcing automatic and professional gaiety, has burdened the able player of Touchstone, Feste, and Lear's Fool with a crushing initial handicap which Shakespeare never intended him to bear. On the contrary, by dressing this character in the coarse, unassuming robe of the lackwit, Shakespeare gives the player an inestimable advantage. Starting under the humble guise of an ordinary idiot, a common butt and familiar laughing-stock, like the ragged little tramp of Charlie Chaplin, the 'fool' can surprise and delight us by deftly and unexpectedly turning the laugh on the laughers.

II. A MOTLEY TO THE VIEW

THE novel and definite knowledge that in Shakespeare's mind's eye a 'motley coat' was an idiot's long coarse robe or childish petticoat of a mixed colour makes us look with new eyes at the phrase 'a motley fool' or simply 'a motley.' We now see that a 'motley' was obviously either an idiot, or else a sane and clever entertainer—whether in private life or on the stage—who adopted the idiot's uniform. This conclusion sends us back to reconsider Shakespeare's lines in Sonnet 110:

> *Alas 'tis true, I have gone here and there,*
> *And made my selfe a motley to the view.* . . .

Here indeed is a personal touch: Shakespeare reflecting on his own behaviour, and in very strong terms. As I thought it over, the temptation to deviate further grew overwhelming, and the present chapter is the result. It is frankly a digression, in which I review the Elizabethan tributes to the excellence of Shakespeare's mind and art. But in the process I uncover evidence which satisfies me that the earliest recorded praise of Shakespeare, both as a man and as an artist, came from the pen of the prince of poets, Edmund Spenser.

If I am not mistaken in my conclusion that Shakespeare composed his Sonnets as a young man, about 1586–1589, during the so-called 'lost years,' his use of 'motley' in the line '*And made my selfe a motley to the view*' may prove to be the earliest recorded example of the word in the sense of 'fool' or 'jester.' But we should not proceed to assume

16

that *to the view* means 'on the playhouse stage.' It is true
that in Sonnet 111, which immediately follows 'a motley
to the view,' Shakespeare clearly reflects on his ill-luck
in that the world allows his worth no better standing than
the humble condition of a stage-player: blaming Fortune

> *That did not better for my life provide,*
> *Then publick meanes which publick manners breeds.*
> *Thence comes it that my name receives a brand,*
> *And almost thence my nature is subdu'd*
> *To what it workes in, like the Dyers hand . . .*

And John Davies of Hereford (in his *Microcosmos*, 1603),
addressing the '*Players*, W[illiam] S[hakespeare] and
R[ichard] B[urbage],' echoes the charge: 'fell *Fortune*
cannot be excus'd That hath for better *uses* you refus'd.'
Yet in spite of this, we must agree with Canon Beeching's
opinion that 'a motley to the view' is not a reference to the
poet's profession as a player. We have no record of stage-
motleys as early as 1589, but in the pageant of ordinary
life a domestic jester who had adopted the idiot's motley
robe must have been a common sight.

What Shakespeare therefore expresses in calling himself a 'motley' is an exaggerated revulsion against his own
perhaps too general and easy success in the company of
his social superiors, in making himself welcome with his
wit and pleasant discourse. As to his appearance, even if
he could not as yet rank as a gentleman, we might expect
to see Shakespeare—as befits a rising and talented actor
—comely, graced in his manners, and perforce hand-
somely dressed. This last surmise finds corroboration in
Sonnet 146, in which he confesses that 'so large a cost' is
spent on keeping his outward man 'rich' and 'so costly
gay.' It is of course grotesque for him to imply that his

welcome as the 'life of the party' made him in any sense a 'motley' or domestic jester in the coarse robe of the lack-wit,

> *esteeméd so*
> *As seelie jearing idiots are with Kings,*
> *For sportive words, and uttring foolish things.*

Donne contemptuously travesties a foolish young gentleman as a 'fondling motley humorist,' and Shakespeare's *Much Ado* presents a similar caricature of the truth in Beatrice's outrageous treatment of the witty Benedick. Pretending not to know him under his mask, she humiliates him by saying of him to his face, 'he is the prince's jester . . . a very dull fool.' In sum, since a 'motley' was a domestic jester in an idiot's petticoat, and was often no more than an amusing half-wit, Shakespeare's self-slander shows even more preposterous than Beatrice's reviling of Benedick.

Humourists who commended themselves by their wit were to be found in all classes of society. Considered from the point of view of social rank, we may take the 'motley' or domestic fool as the gentry's humblest entertainer. (He might of course be one of the well-born 'begged fools'—of whom we shall treat later—but as a certified congenital idiot, a 'fool natural,' he would be treated as a child, a minor, a ward.) At the other extreme we find the high-born voluntary wit at Court, such as Lord Boyet. And though nothing could be clearer than their disparity in rank, the 'motley' and the jesting nobleman might each be not inaccurately described as 'making a fool of himself to make his lord merry.'

It is of the voluntary gentlemen-jesters that John Lyly speaks, apropos the satirical church-reforming 'Martinist' pamphleteer, who remained anonymous but claimed to be a courtier: 'It may be he is some Jester about the Court, and of that I mervaile, because I know all the fooles there, and yet cannot gesse at him.' [1]

Thomas Lodge (*Wit's Miserie*) similarly has no 'motley' in mind in his general satire of 'a jester' in society: 'This fellow in person is comely, in apparell courtly, but in behaviour a very ape, and no man.' In like manner, Ben Jonson's tailor of the times, Fashioner, maintains that good clothes are indispensable in gaining the gentlemen-jesters an ephemeral confidence and success in playing the fool for advantage. Fashioner declares,

> I have had Gallants,
> Both Court and Countrey, would ha' fool'd you up
> In a new suite, with the best wits in being,
> And kept their speed, as long as their clothes lasted
> Han'some, and neate; but then as they grew out
> At the elbowes againe, or had a staine, or spot,
> They have sunke most wretchedly.[2]

In the highest social class, of course, are the rival jesting Lords Berowne and Boyet:

Lady Maria.	That last is *Beroune*, the mery mad-cap Lord. Not a word with him, but a jest.
Boyet.	And every jest but a word.
Princess.	It was well done of you to take him at his word.
Boyet.	I was as willing to grapple, as he was to boord.

(There is more here than the sea-fight quibble. 'To boord'

---

[1] *Pappe with an Hatchet*, Bond's Lyly, III. 397.
[2] *The Staple of Newes* 1.2.

also meant 'to jest.')[1] Berowne puts down Lord Boyet as one who 'pecks up wit as pigeons pease, And utters it again when God doth please.' Representing him as 'holding a trencher, jesting merrily,' he dismisses him as 'allowed'—that is, as a professional jester hired and privileged.

Though Elizabeth's court had no lack of voluntary wits bestirring themselves 'for conceit's sake and to minister occasion of merriment,' decency was not forgotten. Not so under James, where horseplay and the coarser obscenities passed for wit, and knights vied in out-buffooning the professional Fools for their prince's favour. Sir John Finett—later the Master of Ceremonies—wrote bawdy songs for Sir Edward Zouch to sing to James; and, as the contemporary and contemptuous Sir Anthony Weldon has it,

> After the King supped, he would come forth to see pastimes and fooleries; in which Sir Edward Zouch, Sir George Goring, and Sir John Finit were the cheife and Master Fools, (and surely the fooling got them more than any other's wisdome) sometimes present-ing David Droman and Archee Armstrong, the King's foole, on the back of other fools, to tilt one another, till they fell together by the eares: some times they per-formed antick-dances. But Sir John Millicent, (who was never known before) was commended for notable fooling; and was indeed the best extempory foole of them all.[2]

This account of Weldon's has been discounted as libel-lous. There is however reason to believe that he is not

---

[1] 'To boord or jeast, *Bourder, gausser, sorner*' (Cotgrave); 'To boord, or jest, *Jocari, illudere*' (Littleton); 'Boerten, *to Jest, boord*' (Sewel's Dutch–English Dictionary).

[2] Qu. Nichols, *Progresses of James I*, II. 39.

exaggerating the abuse. So notorious grew this blot on the dignity of knighthood, that in their acted plays both Chapman and Day pointed a scornful finger at it:

> A pleasant fellow, 'faith; it seems my lord
> Will have him for his jester: and, by'r lady,
> Such men are now no fools; 'tis a knight's place.
> —*Bussy D'Ambois* (1604), 1.1.196–8.

> *Demetrius.* Was your wit knighted in this last action?
> *Manasses.* I am not such a fool ... I am no knight; I
> am Manasses they made a plain fool.
> —*The Ile of Guls* (1606), 5.1.

The knights' horseplay and gross buffoonery, according to Weldon, 'got them more than any other's wisdom.' Evidently the wisest fool in Christendom felt most at home with the more elementary and barbaric forms of wit. Shakespeare's contemporary efforts to entertain Elizabeth's slovenly successor with the wisdom of *Othello* and of *Macbeth* certainly got him relatively little.

But to get back to Shakespeare in the days of his great Elizabeth after the eclipse of the Armada. No matter what he may say of his own faults, nothing is more certain than that his character kept his behaviour far above that of a Finett or a Zouch. The young poet-actor-playwright's self-disgust in 'I have made my selfe a motley to the view' is of the same attractively excessive kind as Prince Hamlet's 'what a rogue and peasant slave am I!' A neurotic critic, to be sure, might find both utterances neurotic; but it should surprise no healthy mind to discover generous natures unmerciful in self-reproach, and active to condemn even the suspicion of blemish. I should take Shakespeare's self-castigation as meaning no more than 'I have been going out too often, and given my amusing wit too much exercise. People are coming to look upon me as an expected entertainer. I've been a fool to do it.'

Shakespeare's personality draws us irresistibly to him. Since 'the book is the man,' few of his readers can fail to find him not only personally lovable, but admirable as well: of a generous and noble spirit. In him we recognize the Greek *aretê*, defined by Gilbert Murray as 'goodness, high quality, of every kind—artistic skill, courage, generosity, duty: all that makes human life noble.' This is a matter of character, quite independent of the gift of genius. One cannot be reminded too often that Shakespeare's own age, which still held the chivalric ideal, also held him in high regard as a man. His friend Ben Jonson testifies that *the race* (or native disposition)

Of Shakespeares *minde, and manners brightly shines*
  In his well tornéd, and true filéd lines:
In each of which, he seems to shake a Lance,
  As brandish't at the eyes of Ignorance.

Here is the obvious play on *shake spear* that is pictured in his familiar crest or cognizance granted by the College of Arms. More evident to the Elizabethan mind than to ours is the further allusion to Pallas (παλλω, *vibro*), *Dea hastae vibratrix*, the spear-shaking Athena, the arméd goddess of wisdom and of all the arts. In the political cartoon of 1588 on the defeat of the Armada it is as Pallas, in her character of Protector of the State, that the victorious Elizabeth is shown crowned with olive and spear in hand. Again, it is pleasant to note that Shakespeare's charge and crest remind us that his Queen's Nearest Guard, the Band of Gentlemen Pensioners 'extract of noble blood,' was proudly known as *The Spears*.

In granting the crest for the Shakespeare coat of arms, the heralds made *gentility* unmistakable to every Elizabethan eye by choosing a *falcon* to shake the spear.   The 'best and boldest kind of falcon' was the *falcon gentle*. Its lofty spirit and courage inspired the common saying, 'as gentle as a falcon.' The male of this falcon, being a third smaller than the female, was termed the *tercel* or 'tassel.' Shakespeare's Juliet can think of no higher praise for her worshipped lover than to liken him to this noble creature :

> Hist! Romeo, hist! O for a falc'ner's voice
> To lure this tassel-gentle back again!

Worldly rank and Elizabethan notions of 'degree' set aside, men in any age may rightly be ranged and classed according to their spirits in degrees ascending from the churl to the earl, from the plough to the spear. Ben Jonson here gives us Shakespeare as a poet noble in soul, in life, and in utterance: as one of the 'most generous and exalted wits that cannot rest, or acquiesce.' He speaks of him as he was, and can denote him truly. The lines attributed to the Elizabethan Sir Henry Salisbury of Llewenny similarly prize Shakespeare's writings as 'these noble straynes.'

Recognizing as we do the nobility of Shakespeare's spirit, we should not be surprised to find its excellence valued by his contemporaries, who welcomed his wisdom because they saw from what honest and friendly ground it flowered. 'A good life is a main argument.' As Nicholas Rowe justly observed in 1709, Shakespeare's character 'must certainly have inclin'd all the gentler Part of the World to love him.' By 'gentler part' Rowe of course means those of better breeding, the 'gentles' or 'gentility.'

Though we have no real need of their testimony, it is nevertheless delightful to hear those speak out who knew Shakespeare personally; and the burden of their chorus is his spiritual *gentility*. 'Generous yee are in *minde* and *moode*,' declares Davies of Hereford. When Jonson calls him 'honest, and of an open and free nature,' we remind ourselves that *free* connoted the knightly ideal. Duke Orsino, we recall, was 'free, learn'd, and valiant,' and Othello of a 'free and noble nature.' *Gentle* was closely akin to *free*. In considering the epithet 'gentle' we must continually remind ourselves that its meaning has narrowed and weakened since Shakespeare's day. Our modern speech is the poorer without this noble or chivalrous sense of *gentle*, connoting the 'high erected thoughts seated in a heart of courtesy.' No tame connotation of softness is to be found in Volumnia's proud greeting of her warrior son after Corioli as 'My gentle Marcius,' or yet in Miranda's *gentle*, when she warns Prospero to beware how he plays the tyrant with the spirited gentleman Ferdinand:

> O dear fatner,
> Make not too rash a trial of him, for
> He's gentle, and not fearful.

To describe his courteous and fearless Ferdinand and his gentle and noble Brutus in one inclusive epithet, Shakespeare would have had to coin something even better than the French *humble-fier*, which Cotgrave defines as 'mild, well dealt with; stout and froward being abused.'

Sir Philip Sidney's *Arcadia* seemed to Gabriel Harvey 'the silver image of his gentle wit and the golden pillar of his noble courage.' For *gentle wit* we today might say *generous mind*, and set beside it Jonson's word that Shakespeare had 'brave notions and gentle expressions,' meaning *admirable conceptions and noble utterances.* The similar testimony of his old friends Heminges and Cundall, 'Who, as he was a happie imitator of Nature, was a most gentle [magnanimous, spirited] expresser of it,' is joined again by Ben's

> *Yet must I not give Nature all : Thy Art,*
> *My gentle Shakespeare, must enjoy a part.*

At the high-Renaissance court of Elizabeth, was not the chivalrous mark for emulation the 'gentle Sir Philip'? And among the literary followers of 'those noble parts that respect the mind,' it evidently came to be 'gentle Shakespeare.' The praise of contemporaries sounds no similar chorus of 'gentle Marlowe,' 'gentle Daniel,' or 'gentle Drayton.'

This particular appropriation of the epithet to Shakespeare, when placed beside the unequalled height of spirit and expression reached in his Sonnets (written, as I believe, about 1586–1589), calls fresh and sharp attention to an old puzzle: the identity of the poet hailed about 1590 by Edmund Spenser in his *Teares of the Muses* as 'that gentle Spirit.' Shortly afterwards, in his *Colin Clout's Come Home Againe*, Spenser once more greets this poet as '*Aetion*, A gentler shepherd may no where be found.' It was Shakespeare's earliest biographer Nicholas Rowe

who in 1709 first published the conjecture that this
'gentle Spirit' was Shakespeare, as follows: 'the incomparable Mr *Edmond Spencer* . . . speaks of him in his
Tears of the Muses . . . Mr *Dryden* was always of Opinion
that these Verses were meant of *Shakespear*.' But as
modern scholars had not suspected that the Sonnets
might have been completed in 1589, they could not allow
that such early references by Spenser might be intended
for Shakespeare.

Both of the references come shortly after 1589. *The
Teares of the Muses* is included in Spenser's *Complaints*,
entered in the Stationers Register on December 29, 1590.
The printer's epistle speaks of Spenser's 'departure over
Sea,' and Professor F. P. Wilson has shown[1] from Sir
Henry Wallop's account-book for Ireland that Spenser
received a payment there on the preceding May 30, 1590.
Since this represents three months' salary, he may well
have left England before March 1590, and the *Complaints*
were composed at some time before he sailed. In one of
them, Thalia bewails the decadence of comedy in three
allusive stanzas. The first mourns the loss of 'Our
pleasant *Willy*'—the great and genial comedian Tarlton,[2]
who died in September 1588—as 'dead of late':

> With whom all joy and jolly meriment
> Is also deaded, and in dolour drent.

And Spenser goes on to reprehend the piperly playmakers
and make-bates, particularly those of the fierce and scurrilous 'Martin Marprelate' controversy over episcopal
church-government:

---

[1] *Review of Engl. Stud.*, II. 456.
[2] Chambers, *Eliz. Stage*, II. 343.

In stead thereof scoffing Scurrilitie,
And scornfull Follie with Contempt is crept,
Rolling in rymes of shameless ribaudrie
Without regard, or due Decorum kept,
Each idle wit at will presumes to make,
And doth the Learneds taske upon him take.

As one of the tracts (*Martins Months minde*, 1589) testifies, plays certainly formed an element in the counterattack of the orthodox upon the 'Martinists.' The poet-playwrights Lyly and Nashe were in the thick of this noisy fray. Spenser however distinguishes one poet as above selling himself to brawling mockery:

But that same gentle Spirit, from whose pen
Large streames of honnie and sweete Nectar flowe,
Scorning the boldnes of such base-borne men,
Which dare their follies forth so rashlie throwe;
Doth rather choose to sit in idle Cell,
Than so himselfe to mockerie to sell.

This looks to me like a clear reference to Shakespeare. Other writers followed Spenser's lead: 'mellifluous & hony-tongued Shakespeare . . . his sugred Sonnets' (Meres, 1598); '*Shakespeare* thou, whose hony-flowing Vaine' (Barnfield, 1598); 'Honie-tong'd *Shakespeare*' (Weever, 1599); 'Nor doth the siluer tonged *Melicert* Drop from his honied Muse one sable teare' (Chettle, 1603); 'Mellifluous *Shakes-speare*' (Heywood, 1635). If, as I hold, his Sonnets were by this time in circulation, they revealed both the stature of Shakespeare's spirit and the sweetness of his honey-flowing vein. These poems, though passed about 'among his private friends,' were nevertheless at once widely read and imitated,[1] as their author himself tells us in Sonnet 78:

> So oft have I invok'd thee for my Muse,
> And found such fair assistance in my verse,
> As every *Alien* pen hath got my use,
> And under thee their poesie disperse.

But to return to Spenser's praise of 'that same gentle Spirit.' His lines seem to imply that in face of the decadent demand for scurrility, Shakespeare's adherence to his high standard of conduct had for a time put him out of work for the theatre and forced him to sit idle. One cannot be confident that it is from this 'idle Cell' that the young playwright, suffering the spite of Fortune, exclaims,

> Then hate me when thou wilt, if ever, now,
> Now while the world is bent my deedes to crosse. . . .

If however the identification is correct, this is the earliest recognition of Shakespeare on record; and it is gratifying to find Edmund Spenser, 'great Colin, chief of shepherds all,' Sir Philip Sidney's dear friend, leading all the world in paying tribute to the character of the youthful Shakespeare.

So much for Spenser's first allusion. The other one is from *Colin Clout's Come Home Againe*: published 1595, but probably written as a whole in 1591.[2] Here he repeats his high estimate of the 'new' poet's nature, and finds the generous mind reflected in his verse. For after

---

[1] That so-called 'private' poems even reached the press is evident from John Bodenham's anthology from modern poets called *Belvedere*, printed in 1600. Bodenham announced that he drew 'from many of their extant [i.e. published] workes, and some kept in privat [that is, circulated in manuscript].'

[2] Chambers, *William Shakespeare*, II. 187.

passing other poets in review, Spenser concludes with a certain 'Aetion,' unsurpassed for nobility of conception:

> And there though last not least is *Aetion*,[1]
> A gentler shepheard may no where be found:
> Whose *Muse* full of high thoughts invention,
> Doth like himselfe Heroically sound.

Certainly the one poet who 'sounds heroically' is 'Shakespeare.' To make it plainer still, Spenser's 'gentler shepheard' recalls his earlier reference to 'that gentle Spirit,' and both suggest the 'gentle Shakespeare.' When we reflect on the recently-found evidence indicating that his Sonnets—unquestionably 'full of high thoughts invention'—were completed shortly before the date of these allusions, it now appears most probable that Spenser is referring to Shakespeare.

Spenser's use of 'heroically' however raised a doubt in Sir Edmund Chambers's mind that Shakespeare's work (*Venus and Adonis* and *Lucrece*) could be so described, on the assumption that the poet alluded to must have composed in the genre of 'heroic poems.' But Spenser does not say this, any more than he says that the poet is a hero. What he does say is that the poet's 'muse' or poetry, like 'himself' or his name, 'doth heroically sound.' Now, *heroical* in the Elizabethan vocabulary is much like *gentle*: it means *noble* or *magnanimous*. As John Rosse observes (1592, Bodl. MS. Douce 277), 'This well became a mynd heroicall, Inly to greive at others overthrowe.' Similarly, the Spaniard Armado's noble epithet, in likening himself to the 'magnanimous and illustrate' Cophetua, is 'hero-

---

[1] Spenser is taken up by Chambers for scanning the Greek *Aëtion* as trisyllabic. But did he? Surely Spenser may have written 'not least's *Aëtion*', or meant it to be read so.

ical.' We also find Joseph Wybarne reflecting with satis-faction on England's 'many buds of true Nobility, which have brought forth the fruites of Magnanimity and heroy-call vertue' (*The New Age of Old Names*, 1609). And the Elizabethan Gabriel Harvey, on calling the roll of dis-tinguished modern poets, expects 'sum heroical thing' from such 'gentle, noble, & royall spirits.' Both Sidney's *Astrophel and Stella* and Shakespeare's Sonnets, reflecting the nobility of their authors' minds, 'heroically sound.' [1]

If then these allusions of Spenser's clearly point to Shakespeare the sonneteer, the classical name chosen for him by Spenser should certainly likewise contain some recognizable application. What of this name *Aëtion*, applied to the noble-minded shepherd? Sir Edmund Chambers observes that it is a Greek proper name mean-ing 'eaglet,' and quite properly fails to find in the young fowl of tyrant wing any reference to Shakespeare. But to follow linguistic curiosity here may well be to neglect the more obvious approach. Waiving the eaglet of Aëtion as we dismiss the nose of Naso, we should first inquire what Aëtion was known to the Renaissance? And for what was this Aëtion especially renowned? The answers are not far to seek. To the Elizabethans, familiar with Cicero, Pliny, and Lucian in the original or in trans-lation, there was but one Aëtion, an artist celebrated in Lucian's dialogue 'Herodotus or Aëtion.' And he owed his peculiar fame to his marvellous painting, so charmingly described by Lucian, of Alexander's nuptials with Roxana. To illustrate the Elizabethans' familiar knowledge of Aëtion, I find among the Sloane manuscripts a memoran-

---

[1] I find no reference here to the ailment known as 'heroical love' or 'the lover's malady of hereos.'

dum of about 1580 by 'C. S.,' a young Londoner, thus: 'Tabula sive pictura Aëtionis pictoris de coniugio Alexandri magni et Roxanes: habetur in Herodoto vel Aëtione Luciani, q[uod] l[ege]'—'The table or picture by the painter Aëtion of the marriage of Alexander the Great and Roxana: it is in the *Herodotus or Aëtion* of Lucian, which read.'

Let us now try to look at Shakespeare with the eyes of about 1591. The 'gentle Spirit's' impressive achievement in non-dramatic poetry is his Sonnets; and their striking originalities of conception are two. First, they are chiefly addressed not to a beautiful woman, but to a youth.[1] Second, the poet does not, like the rest of the sonneteers, seek to monopolize the object of his affection. On the contrary, he begins by exhorting the youth to marriage; and continues variously and ideally to paint its fruits throughout a series of persuasive pictures.[2] To the early readers of the Sonnets, such as Edmund Spenser, the gentle, heroically-sounding Shakespeare, bringing forth eternal numbers to celebrate the only begetter of his work, stood distinguished as the admirable artist who painted marriage for his 'tenth Muse': in a word, as the latter-day Aëtion.

We have come to the end of our digression. Beginning

---

[1] That the poet's idealizing affection for the young man was not enslaved by the narrower self-absorbed sexualities, both physical and mental, which drive on to the cruder forms of possession and jealousy, is clear enough to any unprejudiced mind both from the frank terms of Sonnet 20 and from the introductory series urging the young friend to marry.

[2] The essential kinship or rivalry between poetry and painting needs no emphasis. Both Horace and Quintilian dealt with it. The poet Simonides called poets 'speaking painters' and painters 'mute poets.' For Petrarch, Homer was the 'first painter of the ancient memories.'

with an attempt to illustrate what Shakespeare meant by saying 'I have made my selfe a motley to the view,' we have been led to consider again what the contemporary view of Shakespeare was. I believe the evidence shows that we must not only include Edmund Spenser among the witnesses both to Shakespeare's character and to his art, but place his tribute as the very first in the list.

III. THE ONLY WEAR

BEFORE our digression we had satisfied ourselves about the true appearance of Shakespeare's stage Fools in motley: they were all dressed, like Elizabethan idiots, in a long coat or petticoat, made of the coarse woollen stuff of a mixed colour, called 'motley,' usually of a dark greenish tinge. The earlier history of this 'motley' cloth makes an absorbing tale, and its main points are well worth recalling.

Even though the traveller Fynes Moryson reported from the Continent in King James's days that a fine motley or 'Kentish' cloth was still fashionable as Court dress in Denmark, we shall find that Shakespeare knew the mingled fabric called *motley* chiefly as a coarse woollen stuff used to make cloakbags or portmanteaux, saddle-covers, barbers' aprons, cheap garments for humble artisans, soldiers' cassocks or gaberdines—and finally, long coats or petticoats (*a*) for 'born fools' or idiots in general, (*b*) for professional domestic fools (whether real lack-wits or clever 'artificials'), and consequently (*c*) for their imitators on the stage.

In Shakespeare's England, the cloth had however come down very far in the world of fashion from the position it had enjoyed in the time of Chaucer, who describes his worthy and stately Merchant as riding 'in motteley.' And early in the reign of Richard II, green motley had been the height of fashion at Court, being worn as summer dress for hunting by the young King and his cousin (and later conqueror) Henry Bolingbroke, Earl of Derby.

The accounts of the Great Wardrobe[1] for the first three years of Richard's reign offer us interesting items. For example, we find the King giving the Earl of Oxford 'a gown and hood parted [that is, parti-coloured in two halves vertically, *halbiert*] of long white russet and green motley cloth for the summer hunting season,' and to the Earl of Derby 'a gown and hood parted of green longcloth and green motley cloth.' Richard himself wore a hunting suit of four garments, of green longcloth and green motley cloth, lined with green taffeta and tartaryn.

Although the King and the Earls, as we have noted, appeared in motley, it is plain that Richard's 'fool of state' did not. 'William Fool,' we read, was suited in a parti-colour of camlet and striped 'caynet' cloth: 'A long tunic, a long tabard and hood parted of short camlet and rayed caynet . . . faced with red, and two pair of breeches . . . for William Fool, by the King's gift.' Certain kinds of 'rayed' or striped cloth (one of which, in the tabard and hood of King Richard's fool, no doubt marks him as a butt) were long used as stigmata of ridicule and contempt. In the generation preceding Richard's reign, an Act of Parliament had decreed that 'no knowne whore should weare any hoode, or attire on her head, except reied or striped cloth of divers colours.'[2] As late as Shakespeare's day, offenders of either sex against the moral code were sometimes condemned to exhibition in a 'ray' hood; and stripes are still penitentiary wear in some parts of the world.

Another of Richard's Wardrobe entries records Philip Walweyn's gift to the King of a summer suit: 'a gown and a hood of chequered motley lined with green taffeta.'

---

[1] P.R.O., E101/400/4.   [2] Kingsford's Stow, II. 166.

This motley doubtless showed a larger pattern, like a fine checked cloth of the present day. The colours of the small squares were green and (perhaps) white, like the fool's fanciful coat-armour described in 1613 by the humourist Robert Anton: 'checkerd *Motley*, Vert and Argent.'[1] By Shakespeare's time, checkered motley had become the professional uniform-apron of barbers, as the following play-quotations make clear; and from the colours of the 'barber's pole' of modern times we may guess that the Elizabethan barber's motley was checkered red-and-white. In John Lyly's *Midas*, barbers are called 'checkerd-apron men.' Beaumont's *Knight of the Burning Pestle* makes the burlesque giant Barbaroso immediately recognizable by his barber's apron: 'he wears A motley garment, to preserve his clothes From blood of those knights which he massacres.' And in Ford's *Fancies, Chaste and Noble*, barbers are set at defiance with the stout declaration, 'I scorne to be jeered by any checker-aproned barbarian of ye all.'

High in favour as it had been in Chaucer's times with Richard of Bordeaux, motley retained its distinguished connotation under Chaucer's follower John Lydgate, as we observe by the envoy of his poem on S. Eadmund. Lidgate here sends forth his humble little work, deprecating its simplicity and crude contrasts, in comparison with the universally admired Cicero's 'motleys'—that is, his fine, sumptuous, and skilfully-mingled colours of rhetoric:

Save black and white, thou hast none other weed;
Of Tully's Motleys, a dark apparence.

---

[1] *Moriomachia*, sig. B4.

It is interesting to find that besides the mingled green motley or 'Kentish,' another familiar woollen cloth, but of *plain* green colour—'Kendal green'—, also had its day of royal favour before sinking so low as to be worn by Falstaff's 'three misbegotten knaves.' Following Edward III's importation of weavers from the Low Countries, this plain green cloth was for centuries made at Kendal in Westmorland and elsewhere. In more modern times the coarser grades became a common dress of the poor. But as late as 1505 the King of Scots had a coat made of it. And it seems that in addition to their plain green, the weavers of Kendal also came to make a motley or 'Kentish' green; for in 1509 we find Henry VIII 'invading the queen's chamber at Westminster "for a gladness to the queen's grace" in the guise of Robin Hood, with his men in green coats and hose of Kentish Kendal.' [1] We recall that Richard II's court had worn green motley for hunting. This record of Henry VIII clearly shows the continued traditional association of green motley or 'Kentish' with hunters and foresters.

From a search of the original Accounts of the Royal Wardrobe, I learn that green motley survived at least to the days of Elizabeth and James as the distinguishing livery of the royal huntsmen—the officers of the Long-bows and the Crossbows, and of the Leash (beagle hounds). To no others of the Household—not even to any of the various Fools, male and female—was any sort of motley issued. The uniform livery of the huntsmen of Elizabeth and James was eight yards of motley for a jerkin or coat: the cloth for the Yeomen and the Grooms of the Longbows, Crossbows, and Leash costing four

---

[1] Chambers, *Medieval Stage*, I. 309.

shillings a yard, and that for the Children of the Leash
(who, by the way, were grown men), three shillings and
fourpence.[1] The Groom of the Privy Buckhounds received 'Kendall' at sixteen pence the yard. These cloths
were among the cheapest issued. The Master Cook, by
contrast, got green cloth and marble cloth (perhaps a
mixture of white, gray, and black),[2] each costing twelve
shillings the yard, three times as much as the better grade
of huntsman's motley.[3]

Relatively cheap as this traditional green motley for
the royal huntsmen was, the kinds known to the ordinary
Elizabethan in soldiers' cassocks, cloakbags, saddle-
covers, idiots' coats, and mechanicals' jerkins were
doubtless cheaper and coarser still.   Lyly has an amusing
dig at the presumption of working-class motley-wearing
Calvinists: 'O what a brave state of the Church it would
be for all Ecclesiasticall causes to come before Weavers
and Wiredrawers, to see one in a motlie Jerkin and an
apron to reade the first lesson!'[4] And in James's reign
the satirical Richard Brathwait ridicules Billy, an upstart
Scottish peasant at the Scottish King's English Court,
who is now to discard his 'aud motley jacket' and strut in
cloth-of-silver.[5]

Motley, then, for royal huntsmen, motley for 'mechanicals,' motley for the Northern peasant. But our chief
concern is with motley for a fool. For the wearing of
congenital idiots, otherwise known as 'innocents' or

---

[1] P.R.O., L.C.5/49/14, 225.
[2] See *A true Relation of Dr. Dee* (1659), 126: 'a Robe like a
Marble colour, spotted white, gray, and black.'
[3] L.C.9/88; A.O.3/1117.
[4] *Pappe with an Hatchet* (1589), *Works*, ed. Bond, III. 405.
[5] *A Strappado for the Divell* (1615), repr. J. Ebsworth, 133.

'naturals,' this humble and cheap covering was most practical. It was durable, and being of a mixed colour would not readily show spots or stains. Brian Melbancke wrote of it as 'A Kentish cloth, That stains with nothing.'[1] The stuff was homely and coarse. Why waste anything better on fools? In his satire on the folly of some of his contemporaries, we find that Roger Sharpe would gladly put them into the idiot's garb which suits their ridiculous ignorance:

> Packe hence ye idle zanies of this age,
> Illiterate fooles, fit subjects for each stage:
> And do not murmur though your coats are course,
> They are too good for fooles if they were worse.[2]

The unpretentious Sculler, the Water-Poet John Taylor, more than once disarmingly pictures his own rimes suitably dressed in the rough garb of fools:

> Plaine home-spun stuffe shall now proceed from me,
> Much like unto the picture of we Three [i.e. Fools].

> No Academicall Poetike straines,
> But homespunne medley of my motley braines.[3]

How far we were astray in our universal error that *motley* was a bright, brave suit of colours is now evident at every turn. Geffrey Whitney, for example, in his moralizing *Choice of Emblemes* (1586), points the contrast for us:

> The ideot likes, with bables [baubles] for to plaie,
> And is disgrac'de, when he is bravelie dreste:
> A motley coate, a cockescombe, or a bell,
> Hee better likes, then Jewelles that excell.

---

[1] *Philotimus* (1583), sig. R3.   [2] *More Fooles Yet* (1610), E3ᵛ.
[3] 'Taylors Farewell to the Tower Bottles,' *Works* (1630), third pagination, 124. *The Nipping and Snipping of Abuses* (1614), sig. B4ᵛ.

In John Ford's play, *The Lady's Trial*, Spinella further implies that 'colours' are no proper dress for a fool, with his advice, 'Do not study, My lord, to apparel folly in the weed Of costly colours.' And in the anonymous play of *Sir Thomas More* (part of which has been attributed to Shakespeare) we have an amusing scene when More, for a joke, has disguised his jester Randall in a gentleman's suit of bright ('painted') colours. After the joke has served its turn, More tells Randall, 'Foole, painted barbarisme, retire thyself Into thy first creation!' In other words, 'Get out of those colours and back into your motley!'

If we inquire what was the commonest predominating hue of the mingled motley fabric, the answer seems to be green: at all events, for the motley appropriated to soldiers' cassocks, to cloakbags, and to fools' coats. We collect evidence of the popularity of green motley for fools from Gabriel Harvey's derision of the playwright John Lyly. Not only does he call Lyly the fiddlestick of Oxford and the very bauble of London, but the Vice-master [or fool-master] of Paul's and Foolmaster of The Theater as well, capping all with an appropriate apostrophe, thus: 'Blessed Euphues, thou only happy, that hast a traine of such good countenances, in thy floorishing greene-motley livery!' [1] Sir William Hollis's idiot-jester or 'flat fool natural,' Jack Oates, as Armin has told us, sometimes wore green motley, sometimes yellow. Shakespeare's Romeo cried down the moon's green livery, on the ground that 'none but fools do wear it.' And in recommending wise behaviour to the old in one of his essays, the youthful Sir William Cornwallis reprobated a 'fantasticness' that 'will dance at threescore yeares olde

---

[1] Grosart's Harvey, II. 226.

and weare Greene and play with a Feather ... it is monstrous and ridiculous, without Hope or Pittie.' We have mentioned the colours of the fool's heraldic coat in the humorous *Moriomachia*, 'checkerd *Motley*, Vert and Argent.' To this, Richard Brathwait chimed in with 'white for *William*, and greene for *Sommer*,' recalling the famous fool of Henry VIII, Will Sommer.[1]

All green things are gay. To suit the folly of 'green minds,' green motley was a clear favourite for pleasant fools. Yellow was, however, also employed; sometimes, as Shakespeare tells us in the passage 'a long motley coat guarded with yellow,' for 'guards' or trimming on the motley coat, sometimes for the whole garment. In satirical vein, the public was reminded that the friends of the idiotic 'Martin Marprelate' should 'mourne for him in gownes and whoods of a bright yellow,' like the fools they were.[2] The Jacobean satirist Barnabe Riche laid it down that 'follies shoulde be ever best suited in a yellow Coate,'[3] and a generation earlier Philip Stubbes had described the Lord of Misrule's men as invested 'with his liveries of green, yellow, or some other light wanton colour.'[4] For evidence of the use of yellow in a later time, Francis Douce, the early Nineteenth-Century authority on the costuming of fools, offers an epigram of 1639 which speaks of 'foole's yellow'; and he even mentions a note from Cromwell's reign holding that yellow was the fool's colour.

As for other and less common hues of motley, at the

---

[1] *The Good Wife*, 1618.
[2] *Martins Months minde* (1589), sig. G1.
[3] *Honestie of this Age* (1614), 50.
[4] *Anatomie of Abuses* (2d ed., 1583).

beginning of the Sixteenth Century there was clearly one in which white predominated. 'The walles shallbe of hauthorne, I wote well, And hanged w^t whyte motly y^t swete doth smell' runs a couplet[1] describing the over-spreading white touched with green and brown. And later in the same century we find a reference to the fall of the white bloom from the hedgerows: 'Hawthorne had lost his motley liverie.' [2]

A brownish motley was also known, to judge by a punning passage in Ben Jonson's *The Case is Altered*, where Aurelia exclaims, 'Why how now sister, in a motley muse? . . . Faith this browne study suites not with your blacke. Your [black] habit and your [brown motley] thoughts are of two colours.' If the brown motley, or dun-coloured spotted cloth, was also worn by 'innocents' or idiots, that connotation may possibly increase our understanding of a couple of instances of 'fool' in Shakespeare, one in *As You Like It* and the other in *A Midsummer Night's Dream*, as follows. We remember that to the compassionate and banished Duke, the speckled dun deer of Arden look like 'poor dappled *fools*,' and that the First Lord likewise calls the stricken and weeping deer 'the hairy *fool*,' and speaks of his '*innocent* nose.' Again, in the *Dream*, does not Bottom see the cuckoo's gray-brown plumage as *the drab motley coat of a bitter taunting fool*, when he calls that tiresome creature with its unpleasing word of fear 'so *foolish* a bird'?

In addition to the motleys called respectively 'green,' 'yellow,' 'white,' and 'brown' motley, there was evidently

---

[1] *Cocke Lorelles Bote* (Percy Soc., 1843), 7.
[2] B.M. MS. Harley 6910, f. 107.

also a 'gray.' The 'aud motley jacket' which, as we have seen, the ambitious Scots peasant Billy would discard on pushing himself in as a courtier under James, was clearly of a gray cast: 'a jerkin of the northerne gray.' [1] Moreover for a Seventeenth-Century Dutch equivalent of 'a Motly colour,' Willem Sewel's *Engels Woordenboek* gives '*Een grove gemengelde, of donker gryze koleur*': a coarse mingled or dark gray colour. We also find indication of a gray motley of mingled black and white (perhaps our familiar pepper-and-salt) in the phrase, 'grim Minos with his motley beard.' [2] And in Massinger's *The Old Law*, Cleanthes asks his old uncle, who has combed his white beard with black lead in order to appear less aged, 'would you . . . change the livery of saints and angels [uniform white] for this mixt monstrousness?' Samuel Butler, the author of *Hudibras*, contributes later evidence of a motley mingled of white and black:

Their poring upon black and white too subt'ly
Has turn'd the Insides of their Brains to motly.[3]

In sum, then, we can produce traces extending from Chaucer's day to Shakespeare's of a number of mixtures, called respectively white, gray, brown, yellow, red-and-white checkered, green, and green-and-white checkered motley. No doubt there were other mingled tints as well; but from many bits of evidence, including the already-quoted letter of the Privy Council, prescribing for soldiers 'a cassocke of motley or other sad green coulor,' it

---

[1] 'A song of a fine Scott,' qu. J. R. Planché, *Inigo Jones* (Shak. Soc., 1848), Introduction.
[2] Verses to Thomas Morton's *New English Canaan*, 1625.
[3] *Remains* (*ca.* 1680) pr. 1759, I. 225, qu. *O.E.D.*

appears unquestionable that the commonest motley was of a dark green shade. It was also the favourite tinge for the fool's motley. In completing our picture of the true appearance of Touchstone, Feste, and Lear's Fool in their long robes of folly, if we give their mixed motley coats a greenish cast, we shall not be far wrong.

IV. A CLOAKBAG FOR A FOOL

'I GOE in Motly making my own cloakebag ready, If hee [i.e. Censure or Criticism] prove porter and beare with me I shall rest behoulding.' To repeat Armin's quip is to observe how neatly it hits off a stock Elizabethan joke. For when a jesting fool grew tedious or offensive, he was banished, hustled away, or carried off like a tiresome piece of luggage, in obedience to the insistent cry, 'Away with the fool!' [1] 'Give us a voyder here for the foole!' [2] 'Take the foole away.' [3] 'Like as a Puppit placéd in a play, Whose part once past all men bid take away.' [4]

Moreover, as we shall see, when anyone's talk proved unbearably silly, the specific call was for *a motley cloakbag*. Heretofore this phrase has conveyed little to our modern ears. But with our new understanding of what *motley* implied, it becomes fascinating. Obviously, a motley cloakbag met the requirements perfectly: providing both motley to coat the manifest fool, and sack or poke to silence and carry the dolt off in. Florio's translation of the Italian *imbaligiare* or *invaligiare* as 'to put up into a Male [mail, sack] or Clooke-bagge. Also to suppresse' calls to mind the trial of the Knave of Hearts in *Alice*, and the

---

[1] Dekker, *Gull's Hornbook* (ed. McKerrow), 52.
[2] *Pilgrimage to Parnassus*, 693.
[3] *Twelfth Night* I. 5. 40.
[4] Spenser, *Mother Hubberds Tale*, 931–2. The Frenchman has much the same idea in his derisory slang phrase, *Au bout du quai, avec les autres ballots!*—Get away to the end of the platform, with the rest of the bundles!

court attendants' businesslike method of 'suppressing' over-enthusiastic guinea pigs.

Thus Armin's declaration 'I goe in Motly making my own cloakebag ready' deftly implies that if he grows tiresome, he can be conveniently carried away as he stands, being already encased in the fool's voluminous coat of cloakbag motley. Not content with this, Armin further turns the laugh on the critics by a witty double play on the sense: (*a*) 'If Censure bear with me, I shall rest beholden'; and (*b*) 'If Censure as a porter bear me in my long motley "cloakbag," I shall rest by holding (being held)';—leaving to the despised porter Censure, like the Devil in the old plays, the labour of carrying off the Fool or Vice.

From judicial records, wills, and inventories, one can readily pick up enough references to motley cloakbags to indicate their commonness in Shakespeare's day: 'a motley cloke-bag worth xij^d'; 'a cloke-bagge of motteley culler'; 'a greene motley Cloakebag'; 'Item one old hempen sheete & one old cloke bagg motely, xvj^d.' [1] As these valuations show, cloakbags of green motley were coarse, cheap, and common. At the other end of the scale, one can find that a portmanteau for the Queen naturally called for materials of a rarer sort: 'Item for making of a Cloake bag of blak vellat layed with lace and lyned with Satten.' [2]

As for 'carrying a man off' in one of these ample

---

[1] *Middlesex Sessions Rolls* (ed. J. C. Jeaffreson), I. 90, 273; Will of Henry Hilton, ostler, 1603, P.P.R. Archd. Lond. Reg. V, 357; Inventory of goods seized at Clopton House by the Bailiff of Stratford upon Avon, Gunpowder Plot, 1606, P.R.O. Exch. Sp. Comm. 4006.

[2] Warrants to the Great Wardrobe, 26 April 1569. B.M. MS. Egerton 2806, f. 14.

baggage-sacks, so far from being absurd, the project was thoroughly practical. To prove it, we are offered a ballad of the time reciting the 'fatall farewell of Captaine Gilbert Horsley [a pirate], conveied [or smuggled] out of ye Counter [Prison] in a clokebag and notwithstanding [rearrested and] condemned for pyracy and executed.' [1]

Obvious and inevitable as this standing Elizabethan joke of 'cloakbag equals fool' now appears, once we understand the likeness of a voluminous green motley cloakbag to the fool's enveloping green motley petticoat, it is curious to observe how frequently it was uttered and has passed by us unappreciated. Here are some of the instances. Stephen Gosson employs it to satirize foolish critics of music, noting that '*Pythagoras* bequeathes them a Cloakebagge, and condemnes them for fooles, that judge Musicke by sounde and eare.' [2] And calling 'Martin Marprelate' an ass ripe for the gallows, the author of *Mar-Martine* counsels him to abandon the disguise of the ordinary citizen's cloak and to stand exposed in the motley which fits his folly: 'Cast of[f] thy cloake and shrive thy selfe, in cloake-bagge, as is meete.' In *Marprelate Epitome* (1589) we find the same taunt again: 'He deserveth to be cased in a good moatley cloakbagg for his labor.'

Thomas Nashe employs the cloakbag at least twice in his writings as a hieroglyph for 'Away with the motley fool!' Once, in derision of a tedious-foolish preacher: 'A man may baule till his voice be hoarse, exhort with tears till his tongue ake and his eyes be drie, repeat that he

---

[1] 19 December 1579. Hyder E. Rollins, 'Analytical Index to Ballad Entries,' No. 871. *Stud. in Philol.* XXI, 80.
[2] *Schoole of Abuse* (ed. Arber), 26.

woulde perswade, till his staleness dooth secretlie call for a Cloake bagge, and yet move no more then if he had been all that while mute.' And again, in the countryman Harvest's rude retort to one who accuses him of resorting to unscrupulous 'fetches' or sharp trading tricks:

Autumne. I, I, such country button'd caps as you
          Doe want no fetches to undoe great townes.
Harvest. Will you make good your words, that we
          want no fetches?
Winter. I, that he shall.
Harvest. Then fetch us a clooke-bagge, to carry away
          your selfe in.
Summer. Plough-swaynes are blunt, and will taunt
          bitterly.[1]

The familiar quip of 'cloakbag for fool' turns up again in William Percy's manuscript play of 1602, *The Aphrodysial*, 3.7. Here the water-nymph Humida, whom Vulcan has annoyed with unmannerly love-making in the presence of his cyclops-servant Harpax, threatens to 'blazon' the blacksmith-god with disgrace before Cytherea: and the servant Harpax gleefully interrupts with, 'In a Mottley, I beseech you, Lady—And mee to provide the cloak-bag for him.' George Chapman's Angelo (in his comedy *May-Day*) further rings the changes on the favourite jest, slyly calling Lorenzo a fool in a variety of ways: 'for say you were stuffed into a motley coat, crowded into the case of a base viol, or buttoned up in a cloak-bag even to your chin, yet if I see your face, I am able to say, "This is Signor Lorenzo."'

If for a moment we turn from the playwrights to the

---

[1] *Works* (ed. McKerrow), I. 45, and III. 262.

divines, we are diverted to find Dr. William Laud (President of St. John's College, Oxford, not yet a bishop) interrupting his work long enough to relieve his feelings about certain tiresome University officials. To accommodate such learned asses and wise idiots, he thoughtfully draws up a prospectus for a suitable institution, 'Gotam College,' naming among the 'benefactors' the noted fools Will Sommer, Charles Chester, Patch, and Bubble. In his rules and regulations for this ideal fatuous foundation, Laud prescribes for the students the following under *Apparel*: 'Wear . . . no breeches but motley, and are therefore to have all old cloak-bags given them to help the poorer sort.' [1]

Finally, in the Cambridge University play *2 Return from Parnassus*,[2] the clever Ingenioso handles the joke under two forms. First he observes that there are no fools like over-dressed satin-and-velvet dandies; but that fortunately contemporary satirists (like clever tailors) have exposed them for the tedious fools they are, by showing them fit to be carried off in their more suitable 'cloakbag' motley: 'There is no foole to the Sattin foole, the Velvet foole, the perfumde foole; and therefore the witty Taylors of this age put them under colour of kindnesse into a paire of cloakbagge breeches, & so the fooles are taken away in a cloakbagg, where a voyder will not serve the turne.' Ingenioso's second passage is simpler: 'you that hate a scholler, because he descries your Asses eares; you that are a plagie stuffed Cloake-bagge of all iniquitie,

---

[1] Quoted from S. P. Dom. by John Bruce, *Notes & Queries*, 3d. S., V. 1–5. Compare *The statutes and constitutions of Gotam College, or The Hospitall of Fooles*, in Mabbe's 1622 translation of Aleman's *Guzman*, Pt. 2, Bk. 3, Ch. 1.

[2] Ed. J. B. Leishman, lines 1575–80, 1655–59.

which the grand Serving-man of Hell will one day trusse up behind him, and carry to his smokie Ward-robe . . .' *Plaguy stuffed cloakbag of all iniquity* here plainly suggests both fool and knave, like that old favourite trouble-and-fun maker, the Vice or 'Iniquity' of the Morality plays. In his *Whip for an Ape* (another attack on 'Martin Marprelate') John Lyly offers the apish 'Martin' the stage Vice's role, vacated by the death of the great comic, Tarlton:

> Now *Tarleton's* dead the Consort lacks a vice:
> For knave and foole thou maist beare prick and price.

We have seen enough to understand by now how naturally, and indeed inevitably, the Elizabethan mind linked *cloakbag* with *motley fool*. If with our new knowledge we consider Shakespeare's old Jack Falstaff, dismissed by the crowned and altered Hal with the cutting words, 'How ill white hairs become a fool and jester!' our thoughts hark back to a happier time when Hal's insults were given with a smile. And now we realize that as well as styling old Jack 'that reverend Vice,' Hal had also, in the phrase 'that stuffed *cloakbag* of guts,' genially miscalled him a fat *motley fool*.

Characteristically sportive, our Elizabethans spread the joke by a kind of counterpoint from 'cloakbag' to its synonyms—sack, baggage, and poke. Initiated into the mystery of 'cloakbag is motley fool,' our eyes are now opened to the corollary quips. By way of example we note that Lyly, whom we have seen prescribing A Whip for an Ape—the disguised knave-and-fool 'Martin Marprelate'—, also taunts him as follows with 'sack' and 'baggage':

49

A Dizard[1] [idiot] late skipt out upon our Stage;
But in a sacke, that no man might him see . . .
Who knoweth not, that Apes men Martins call;
Which beast this baggage seems as t'were himselfe . . .

With this light it becomes plain that when Shakespeare
likewise says 'sack,' he also means 'fool.' In *Love's
Labour's Lost* (4.3) we have a quartet of folly, when all
four forsworn gentlemen, having let themselves be cap-
tured by Cupid, betray themselves as a mess of fools in
love, 'four woodcocks in a dish.' The King confesses himself a fool, Berowne brands himself and Longaville fools;
and when Dumaine appears in the same transformation,
Berowne's cry, from the old children's game, is 'More
sacks to the mill!'—that is, 'another sad sack of fool's
motley!'

In addition to these nicknames 'cloakbag' and 'sack' for
the fool's motley cover-all, I believe another one has lain
concealed in a familiar passage from *As You Like It*.
Recounting his first meeting with Touchstone, Jaques recalls how the 'motley fool' then 'drew a dial from his
poke, And looking on it with lack-lustre eye, Says very
wisely, "It is ten o'clock." ' Our question is, what was
Touchstone's 'poke'? For lack of information, the commentators take it to be a 'a small pocket' somewhere in his
clothes. But the only meanings for *poke* recorded in the

---

[1] '*Bamba*, a dizzard or naturall foole' (Percivale-Minsheu). '*Fol*,
a foole . . . dizard . . . naturall, ideot' (Cotgrave). '*Balordo*, a
dizzard, a giddie-head, by met. simple and foolish. *Zurlo*, a giddi-
nesse or dizzinesse in the head. Also a gull, noddy or ninny'
(Florio).

For *sack*, see Florio's definition of *Larva*: 'according to Bocace,
a kinde of upper garment like a Porters frock or sacke, or such sacks
as tumblers tumble in.'

Oxford English Dictionary down to the date of Shakespeare's play are 'bag,' 'long wide or full sleeve,' 'bagnet' (for fish), and 'goitre.' The last three of these are obviously special senses of 'bag.'

Pokes in Shakespeare's time commonly were bags of ample proportions, as indeed they are today, 'holding a definite quantity varying according to the nature of the commodity, as wool, coal, meal, hops.' A *sack* of wool, for instance, held 26 stone (364 pounds), giving the 'comparative' Hal his term for Falstaff: 'How now, woolsack?' A *poke* of wool held half a sack, or 182 pounds—more nearly the weight of a natural man. And as for 'meal pokes,' who could forget the capacious maw of the Miller of Enfield's 'great Poake,' in the ironical *Defence of Conny Catching*, which devoured the flour he stole in the grinding? Hop pokes, still common in Kent and elsewhere, are huge cylindrical bags holding ten bushels. As everybody knows, a poke will contain and conceal a marketable pig;—even two actively wallowing pigs, according to Chaucer: 'they walwe as doon two pigges in a poke.' Finally, we note that some uses of the word significantly identify *poke* with our Elizabethan *cloakbag*: there is the charming old Scots term for portmanteau, *pokemantie*, and in Virginia travelling-bags are still known as 'go-pokes.'

With the fool's motley 'cloakbag' and 'sack' freshly in mind, we now see somewhat more in Touchstone's 'poke.' When Jaques (who pretends to envy Touchstone his motley coat) mentions the fool's 'poke,' he is merely varying the well-worn joke on the fool's motley cover-all cassock, otherwise known as his 'sack' or 'cloakbag.' Evidently, if Feste can *impetticoat* a gratuity, Touchstone may be allowed to *epoke* his dial.[1] As for the receptacle or *pocket* for Touchstone's timepiece inside his 'poke,' it was no doubt what the Spaniards called a *falsopeto*: 'a pocket in the bosome, such as priests use in their cassocks or frocks to carry their handkerchiefs or booke in.' Indeed, the priest in *Twelfth Night* must have thus carried his watch, drawing it out near the close of the play to observe, 'Since when, my watch hath told me, toward my grave I have travell'd but two hours.'

When we begin exploring the riches of Shakespeare's language, one thing inevitably leads on to another. It was wondering about 'motley' which at length produced a clear picture of the authentic stage-appearance of Shakespeare's Fools. It was looking at the coarse robe of mingled colour that covered them which inevitably revealed the point of the puzzling joke about 'cloakbag.' Then the cloakbag carried us along, *via* Falstaff, not only to the four 'sacks' of folly in *Love's Labour's Lost*, but finally to the long motley 'poke' in which Touchstone delighted Jaques. Shakespeare left all this humorous luggage plainly marked, but we are only now claiming it.

---

[1] Though usually glossed 'sun dial,' this is more likely to have been a mechanical watch. Cf. 'one houre dial commonly called a watch'—Anno 1611, in *Whorwood v. Gifford*, P.R.O. Req. 2/364.

V. PETTICOAT FOR PRIVILEGE

THE 'motley' *material* of the Shakespearean Fool's costume is by this time fairly clear in our minds. Let us now for a change put the emphasis not on the cloth, but on the shape or form of the Fool's dress. For having pretty thoroughly forgotten Douce the costume-historian's conclusion that the 'allowed fool' or official domestic jester was generally habited in a long petticoat—and beguiled by our mistaken and misleading romantic picture of Shakespeare's Fool in medieval parti-coloured clothes —we have been far from realizing how universally prevalent and customary this long coat or surtout was for the costume of the Elizabethan domestic fool. Yet testimony to the fact has always been at hand in abundance. To Shakespeare's voluble fellow-author Nashe it seemed a matter of common knowledge: 'fooles, ye know, alwaies for the most part (especiallie if they be naturall fooles) are suted in long coates.'[1] So familiar to the Elizabethans was the figure they cut in their long coat, that we find the notion applied as an insult to one of the royal officers wearing his regular long livery coat. For in 1592 we have a Messenger of the Queen's Chamber complaining in court that a contemptuous serving-man called him 'foole and Jack A napes, and badd him gett out of the dores with his fooles cote on his backe.'[2]

Shakespeare's text presents actual evidence hitherto unnoticed, showing that it was in this skirted dress that his

---

[1] Epistle to *Have With You*. McKerrow's Nashe, III. 17.
[2] *Gill v. Hanbury*, Easter 34 Eliz. P.R.O. Req. 1/199.

fellow-actor Armin 'created' all three of the stage characters of Touchstone, Feste, and Lear's Fool. We have long known, from the frontispiece of Armin's own play *Two Maids of More-clacke* (1609), that he wore it when acting Blue John, the contemporary adult idiot-protégé of Christ's Hospital, the main interest of his play. The stuff of Armin's long coat in this role would naturally be that of the familiar woollen 'bluecoat' of the boys of the Hospital. For his coats when he appeared as Shakespeare's fools, on the other hand, the material was the coarse woollen cloth of mixed colour called 'motley.'

To the professional fool in private life, whether he were a congenital lack-wit 'natural,' or a clever 'artificial' playing the simpleton, the useful significance of the long robe (being the recognized uniform of the idiot) was the licence, indulgence, or privilege allowed to the innocent and irresponsible. 'Fools only speak *Cum Privilegio.*' In Davenant's play *News from Plymouth* an insolent antagonist is called to account with the angry warning, 'You weare no Petticoat for priviledge!' And when Fletcher's Roderigo, in *The Pilgrim*, sees Alinda disguised as an idiot, he exclaims, 'The devil in a fool's coat? is he turn'd innocent?'

We need hardly recall in passing that in other groups in society the long coat or petticoat was then—and still is today—associated with a special, privileged, or protected status. Women are an obvious instance of this. Dressed as a man, Rosalind reminds herself, 'But I must comfort the weaker vessel [Celia], as doublet and hose ought to show itself courageous to petticoat.' In Nathan Field's *Amends for Ladies*, Lady Bright, after boldly subduing her intending ravisher with a sword, tells him, 'You'll hold a

more reverent opinion Of some that wear long coats.'
And in Dekker's *Roaring Girl*, Sir Alexander Wengrave
sees the world turned upside down: 'What age is this! if
the wife go in breeches, the man must wear long coats
like a fool.' Volpone's hermaphrodite fool or jester
Androgyno inevitably appears in the long woman-like
dress. Likewise, when the hero of Fletcher's *Monsieur
Thomas*, clad in woman's clothes, is about to make up his
match with Mary, she naturally calls him 'fool' because of
his skirts; whereupon he incontinently discards the 'fool'
or 'woman' which covers his man's attire:

Mary.   Come foole; I am friends now.
Thomas. The foole shall not ride ye,
           There lye my woman, now my man again.

Dressed in the soutane, frock, or cassock of their profession, priests similarly were privileged persons. In
Henry VIII, Lord Surrey tells Wolsey, 'Your long coat,
priest, protects you; thou shouldst feel My sword i' the
the life-blood of thee else.' And the Scots, we are told,
had a similar threatening saying as a proverb 'spoken
when Clergymen use you Saucily, whom, in deference to
their profession, you will not beat,' as follows: 'Many
ones coat saves their doublet.' [1] Great is the power of the
long coat or skirt! Even today it is notable, for we hear
that in Madrid 'the armed police . . . are dressed in long
grey womanish overcoats. So that it is said that Spain
today is run by the three skirts—the police, the priests,
and the women.' [2]

So much for the robes, long coats, or petticoats, of

[1] Kelly, *Scot. Prov.* (1721), 251; qu. *Oxf. Dict. Engl. Prov.*, 287.
[2] Honor Tracy in *The Listener*, March 2, 1950, p. 369.

women, priests, and policemen. Now to return to those
of 'innocents' proper in Shakespeare's time. The petticoat, we find, was inescapably part of the Elizabethan
mental picture of an idiot. For even when they thought
of an ancient Roman pretending to be an idiot, they would
clothe him in their mind's eye with their own fool's
familiar long coat. In proof of this, we have Shakespeare
(both in *Henry V* and in *The Rape of Lucrece*) describing
what the classical Junius Brutus put on when he simulated idiocy to avert suspicion while plotting the death of
Tarquin the tyrant. In *Henry V* he calls it 'a Coat of
Folly,' and in *Lucrece*, 'that shallow habit,' as follows:

Constable [speaking of King Harry].
> And you shall find, his Vanities fore-spent,
> Were but the outside of the Roman *Brutus*,
> Covering Discretion with a Coat of Folly.

[Brutus] Began to cloath his wit in state and pride,
> Burying in Lucrece wound his follies show.
> He with the Romains was esteeméd so
> As seelie jearing idiots are with Kings,
> For sportive words, and uttring foolish
> things.
> But now he throwes that shallow habit by,
> Wherein deepe policie did him disguise.[1]

And despite all his classical learning, Ben Jonson likewise joined with his audience in a mental picture of this
same Junius Brutus disguised in an Elizabethan fool's long
coat, as we notice in *Bartholomew Fair*. Here, when
Justice Overdo comes on—'a Justice in the habit of a
foole'—wrapped in what he calls his 'cloud' or 'cover-

---

[1] *Henry V*, 2.4.36–38; *Lucrece*, 1809–15.

ing,' he spurs himself forward to duty with 'On, Junius Brutus!'

The derivation of the long coat for the lack-wit or 'natural' is plain. It had been very naturally borrowed or retained from the contemporary dress of 'babes' or little boys. Gascoyne the poet speaks of 'boyes which wear such side long gowns.' ('Side' meant 'long.') In writing the life of Ben Jonson for his *Worthies* (1662), Thomas Fuller tells us, 'Though I cannot ... *find him* in his *cradle*, I can *fetch him* from his *long coats*.' Richard Brathwait, in his *Spirituall Spicerie* (1638) recalls his own childhood: 'Now when I found myselfe growne from my coate ...' And Shakespeare's Pedro (in *Much Ado*) says it is an affront 'to show a child his new [long] coat and forbid him to wear it.' When Falstaff of *The Merry Wives* cashiers Nym and Pistol, retaining only the long-coated little Robin, his word is 'French thrift, you rogues— myself and skirted page.' Nashe, in his *Pierce Penilesse*, lumps the costumes of children and fools together, lamenting the fact that 'we divide Christ's garments ... and ... make some of us Babies and apes [i.e. fools'] coates.' Boys' coats closely resembled fools' coats not merely in shape, but often in being similarly 'guarded' or trimmed near the hem with ornamental bands or 'guards.' In Marston's play *Histriomastix* we hear of naughty boys presuming on their similarity of costume to play the mocking fool. The result is a whipping: 'Rascall boyes, Who Ape-like jet [strut], in guarded coates; are whipt For mocking men.' The hero of Chapman's *Monsieur D'Olive* pointedly tells some saucy pages they are little idiots, in these words: 'Well, I perceive Nature has suited your wits [that is, made you 'naturals' or idiots], and I'll suit you in guarded coats, answerable to your wits; for [a fool's] wit's as suitable to [fools'] guarded coats as wisdom is to [scholars'] welted gowns.'

Domestic fools and little boys often shared another piece of equipment in addition to the long coat. This was the dagger, worn at the back, suspended from the girdle.[1] It was usually wooden (sometimes gilded), like the dagger of lath wielded by the knavish Fool or Vice of the Morality plays. In *The Divell is an Asse* Ben Jonson introduces an old-time Vice named 'Iniquity,' who recalls that about the year 1560 'every great man had his *Vice* [meaning his domestic jester] stand by him, In his long coat, shaking his wooden dagger.' *The Winter's Tale* shows us King Leontes calling to mind the figure he himself presented as a child before graduating into breeches: 'unbreech'd, In my green velvet coat, my dagger . . .' And in *Christmas his Masque* Jonson prescribes the costume for the character Baby-Cake, *alias* Child Rowlan: '*Drest like a Boy, in a fine long Coat, Biggin* [cap], *Bib, Muckender* [handkerchief hung in girdle], *and a little Dagger.*' (The muckender or mucketer—Ital. *moccatore*, from *moccare*, 'to snuffe or blowe the nose'—was that conveniently-placed means of wiping the fool's or child's nose or mouth which appears prominently in the frontispiece to Armin's play, showing him dressed as the idiot Blue John.[2]) The court fool Raphe Simnel is brought on the stage by Robert Greene in similar equipage: 'Marrie, Sirha Ned,' says Raphe to the Prince, 'thou shalt put on my cap and my coat, and my dagger.'[3] In *The Noble*

---

[1] 'The woodden dagger may not be worne at the backe when S. Paules sword, hangs by the side.'—*Martins Months minde* (1589), D2ᵛ. [2] See page 102. [3] *Friar Bacon and Friar Bungay*, 1.1.31.

Gentleman, Fletcher and Rowley's character Longaville suggests attire appropriate to the folly of Monsieur Mount-Marine: 'According to his merits, he should wear A guarded coat, and a great wooden dagger.' Chapman's Maffé in *Bussy D'Ambois*, imagining Bussy to be a new jester at court, mentions his 'wooden dagger.'

The dagger had been so long and so closely identified with the fool that it may well have provided the name for the Arthurian jester, Sir Dagonet. Cotgrave's French and English Dictionary (1611) gives 'a little dagger' for the French word *daguenet*. The Elizabethans borrowed 'Sir Dagonet' as a favourite by-name for a fool. 'When I lay [as a student] at Clement's Inn—I was then Sir Dagonet in Arthur's show' is the boast proper to foolish old Shallow. Nor is Sir Dagonet neglected by Ben Jonson. Of the rich sloven Sogliardo and the sharking Shift in *Every Man out of His Humour* the scurrilous Carlo Buffone exclaims, 'gods so, looke here, man; Sir *Dagonet*, and his squire!' And when the ridiculous Puritan glutton Zeal-of-the-Land Busy addresses a squeaking puppet in *Bartholomew Fair* as 'Dagon,' the outraged idol retorts on him with '*What then, Dagonet?*' In *Cynthia's Revels*, Crites scornfully refers to the impudent Anaides as 'your fellow, sir *Dagonet*, here.' Beaumont's play *The Knight of the Burning Pestle* exhibits the simple-minded grocer, Citizen George, claiming King Arthur's fool as a member of his own trade, demanding, 'I pray you, what was Sir Dagonet? Was he not prentice to a grocer in London?' And Davenant's Ginet, in *The Wits*, says of two ridiculous fellows, 'I'd lose my wedding to behold these Dagonets.'

Even the Fool who was a feature of the traditional

Morris dance, and who had his own distinct ancestry, sometimes wore the long dress, as Nashe implies in his *Pasquil and Marforius*, ridiculing Giles Wigginton the Calvinist church-reformer. Presenting Wigginton dressed as the lewd Morris fool, Nashe says, '*Wiggenton* daunces round about him in a Cotten-coate [i.e. of woollen-frieze], to court him with a Leatherne pudding [sausage] and a woodden Ladle.' [1] And Lyly satirically shows us John Udal, another 'Marprelate' champion, in a similar robe: 'he sate writing in a fooles coate, & so he was caught and whipt.' [2]

All these Elizabethan figures, whether of childish years, feeble mind, or clever artificial fooling, present one constant feature of costume—the long coat or petticoat dress. And though other styles in costume altered, we find that the long coat for fools far outlasted the Elizabethan age. In a play of 1640—which seems to foreshadow the marching, the soldiers' gaberdines, and the battle-smoke of the imminent Civil Wars—we read that playgoers 'have nothing for their money but a Drumme, a Fooles Coat, and Gunpowder.' [3] And when after a raid on the 'suppressed' playhouses during the wars a suggestion was made in the Commons that the soldiers might have the confiscated costumes, 'H[arry] M[artin] stood up, and told the Speaker that . . . he feared they would fall out for the *Fool's Coat*.' [4] In June 1652 the scribbler of the satirical news-pamphlet *Mercurius Democritus* claimed to have 'spy'd a fellow in a long fools coat a hors-back upon a Bull.' [5]

---

[1] McKerrow's Nashe, I. 83.   [2] Bond's Lyly, III. 403.
[3] Lewis Sharpe, *The Noble Stranger*, sig. G3^v.
[4] Thomas Forde, *Faenestra in Pectore* (1660), 50.
[5] B.M. E669.17.

Even after the Restoration we note an interesting survival of Shakespeare's stage practice, when the playwright Davenant took the foolish step of crushing
Measure for Measure and *Much Ado* into a single 'new'
play called *The Law against Lovers*. This was certainly
'out of two good plays to make one bad,' but Davenant
(who was ten years old when Shakespeare died) drew on
his personal knowledge of how the original plays were
staged; and his monstrous adaptation preserves significant vestiges. For example, in *Measure for Measure*, when
the foolish bawd Pompey is brought in by the officers on
the way to prison, the text shows that he is fettered, for
Constable Elbow says, 'His neck will come to your waist
—a cord, sir.' At this same point Davenant's adaptation
gives the stage direction *Enter Fool in a Shackle*. Immediately after this, Davenant provides a revealing touch in
Lucio's speech: "Fool! what, a Pris'ner? . . . A Bawd in a
Fools Coat?' Thus, in presenting the fool-and-bawd in a
long coat, Davenant is doubtless merely continuing
Shakespeare's practice in costuming Pompey like a fool.
It has perhaps not been generally recognized that, besides
Pompey, Shakespeare in *Timon of Athens* presents a re-
lated character of similar class and costume: the harlot's
fool. This 'fancy man,' because of his (wooden) side-
arms and his long motley coat, reminiscent of the cassock
or gaberdine of the soldier, is jestingly addressed as
'Captain.' (For the same reason of military resemblance,
King Leontes in *The Winter's Tale* playfully calls his
child Mamillius, with his long coat and dagger, 'Captain.')
Actually, of course, this base hired lover or whore's
'bully' is poles apart from an honourable captain, except
in a superficial resemblance of dress. But with his figure

in mind, we at length perceive the aptness and the low connotations of Philo's vile name for his lust-slaved stallion captain, Mark Antony: 'strumpet's fool.'

As a feature of our new-old costume-picture, we have already noted that the fool's long coat, as Shakespeare tells us, was sometimes 'guarded': that is, ornamented in a contrasting colour near the hem with one or more encircling, laid-on strips or bands, usually of velvet (see Frontispiece). *Double-guarded* and *triple-guarded* signified two and three guards or bands. It is a cassock trimmed in this fashion which Thomas Kyd's Erastus promises to the fool Piston, in *Soliman and Perseda*: 'a guarded suit from top to toe'; and it is also the 'good case' on which John Marston's Malevole compliments the fool Passarello in *The Malcontent*: 'You are in good case since you came to court, fool; what, guarded, guarded!' In *Bartholomew Fair*, Ursula and Wasp describe Justice Overdo's 'Mad Arthur of Bradley' disguise as a 'guarded coat.' Richard Brathwait's 'The Cuckow' (printed 1658 with his *Hon.st Ghost*, but written some years earlier) pictures Virtue in the garb of a domesticated lack-wit:

And thus must *vertue* do, or *shee* must sterve;
For *Idiot*-like (poore foole) shee's bound to serve
In garded coat, or such like Liverie,
Or die in want, exposed to miserie.

A contemporary woodcut of the character Antonio (in the title-role of Middleton and Rowley's *Changeling*) shows him disguised as a 'gentle nigget' or tame idiot in a long fool's coat for the purpose of wooing Isabella unsuspected. In the dialogue he tells her, 'This shape of folly shrouds your dearest love'; but later, when she also feigns madness, and he fails to see through her disguise, she scornfully counsels him, 'Keep your caparisons, you're aptly clad.'

While the cut of the fool's coat never changed, being always long, Elizabethan styles in gentlemen's clothes, on the other hand (like our modern women's fashions), exhibited their pendulum-swings or revolutions from long to short, and from short to long.[1] It was when the extreme fashion decreed 'long' that the satirists of extravagance in costume naturally had their innings. For then they promptly and pointedly likened the 'new look' to the perennial long coat of the fool. For example, that the 'long' was in vogue about the year 1597 (though expected soon to give way to the 'short') appears by an amusing interchange between Thomas Nashe and Richard Lichfield, each busily tailoring a garment of satire for the other. Thus Nashe offers Lichfield something nice and long like a fool's coat, and Lichfield retorts (in *The Trimming of Thomas Nashe*) as follows:

'Where thou commendest thy Epistle to me as a garment for a fool, and therefore that it should be long ... yet I have made thy coat short and little ... wear it and use it well, for the fashion of long clothes is wearing away, and short clothes will shortly be in request again, and then thou shalt be a fool of the fashion as soon as the proudest of them all.'

---

[1] See Henry Peacham's reflection on fashions in *The Worth of a Penny* (1647): 'That emblem was not improper which I saw at Antwerp, where was a he-fool and a she-fool turning a double-rimmed wheel upon one axle-tree, one on the one side and the other on the other. Upon the he-fool's wheel were the several fashions of men's apparel; on the other wheel, of women's; which with the revolution of time, went round, and came into the same place, use, and request again; as for the present aloft, and followed of all, by and by, was cast down and despised.'

Despite Lichfield's confident prediction, the 'long' fashion in gentlemen's wear seems to have held on—and with exaggerations—into 1598. For in his *Scourge of Villanie* of that year, Marston names a certain *Pyso* as a fashion-leader in popularizing doubtlets or jerkins so elongated as to expose them to comparison with fools' coats, huge breeches or 'slops,' and boots with 'ears' or 'lugs':

> For not a fashion once dare show his face,
> But from neate *Pyso* first must take his grace.
> The long fooles coat, the huge slop, the lugg'd boot
> From mimic *Pyso*, all doe claime their roote.

If the hand of fashion's dial dropped to 'short' in the interim, by 1609 it must have pointed once more to 'long,' for Acutus in *Everie Woman in her Humor* (1609) says he grieves 'to see this double-garded age, all side-coate [long coat], all foole.' Twenty years after this again, in 1629, an observer is likewise stirred to ironical praise of the devotees of the extreme 'long,' who 'have attained ... the verie true habite of naturall simplicitie and true idiots, covering their whole bulke, ... from heade to heeles, with long side-coates such as was the noble Archie's, our late Sovereigne's Jester (save that his was of velvett, and theirs are of cloth).' [1]

James's Fool, Archibald Armstrong, here naturally brought on the scene, seems always to have worn the 'petticoat for privilege': made, however, not of the coarse motley woollen, but of velvet. In this expensive dress the 'principal fool of state' was certainly extraordinary, but

---

[1] 'A Relation of Some Abuses,' pr. F. Madden, *Camden Misc.*, 1855.

perhaps not unique. For we must recognize that Samuel Rowlands (in *A Fooles Bolt*, 1614) finds it possible to imagine a merry fool at a fair, 'in his best fools-clothing neate: Thrusting amongst them in a velvet Coate, Downe to the Anckles.' And again in Marston's *Malcontent* there is an amusing dialogue on the subject of such finery for a domestic fool, between Bilioso, 'an old choleric marshal,' and Bianca:

Bil. Passarello, my fool . . . shall be in velvet.
Bian. A fool in velvet!
Bil. Ay, 'tis common for your fool [i.e. foolish gentle-man] to wear satin. I'll have mine in velvet.
Bian. What will you wear then, my Lord?
Bil. Velvet too; marry, it shall be embroidered, be-cause [i.e. so that] I'll differ from the fool somewhat.

In Tudor and Stuart times it was not only the English who covered their fools with petticoats and their court fools occasionally with velvet. Cotgrave cites a French equivalent for 'ninny' or fool as *Jan gipon* or *jan-gippon*: that is, *Jean Jupon*, or, as we might say, Petticoat John; and the wardrobe of Marguerite of Navarre's jester Guérin included '*une robe de velours, une soutane de satin noir avec un bonnet carré.*' [1]

In the passage just given from *The Malcontent*, Bianca's surprise at velvet for Marshal Bilioso's fool nevertheless reflects the normal view. Fools were commonly clothed not in ostentation, but in 'the napless vesture of humility.' For the silly jeering idiot's petticoat, velvet or satin might be the rare exception, but woollen motley was the rule, as the following quotations make clear. In Middleton's

---

[1] Quoted in Miss Enid Welsford's *The Fool*, 156.

Mayor of Quinborough, Mayor Simon orders the player-clown to dress for the performance: 'Away, then; shift, clown, to thy motley crupper'—as though in his flowing caparisons he were a barded steed whose long trapping trailed from its rump. Ben Jonson similarly pictures the fulness of the fool's robe in the sentence passed on the foolish Matheo: to stand bound at the market cross 'in a large motlie coate.'[1] Also coated in the customary long woollen motley was Leonard, the 'lean fool' of the sottish half-dozen in Robin Armin's book *Foole upon Foole*: 'motly warm, Ever went leane Leonard.' *Warm* here implies, of course, the *woollen* coat. (To modern ears the epithet recalls the familiar name of the Army overcoat, 'British Warm.') 'Warm' also shows us the figure in long woollen coat which an untalented buffoon cut in the mind's eye of Hamlet, as he remarked, 'God knows, the warm Clown cannot make a jest unless by chance.'

Lean Leonard, Armin tells us, always went 'motley warm'—thus neatly giving the lie to the saying that a fool has not wit enough to keep him warm. 'In motley coats goes Jack Oates,' Robin Armin also sings of Sir William Hollis's celebrated 'natural,' 'flat fool,' or 'fool positive'; and so likewise go Shakespeare's three leading fools portrayed by the same jolly Robin upon the stage. We have already seen that 'a long motley robe like Touchstone's' is what Jaques meant by saying 'I am ambitious for *a motley coat*,' and also in his tale of how the Fool 'drew a dial from his *poke*.' As for Feste's costume, ever since Dr. Johnson explained 'impeticos' as 'impetticoat,' it should have been evident to all that for this fool, too, Shakespeare clearly indicates the motley petticoat when he has Feste

---

[1] *Every Man in his Humour* (Quarto, 1601), 5.3.360.

say, 'I did impeticos [put into my petticoat] thy gratillity [gratuity]' and 'I wear not motley in my brain [as I do on my back].' May I in passing suspect Feste of a possible further corrupting of words in this same report on the modest tip with which the wealthy Sir Andrew had all too gently scratched his itching or impetiginous palm? Why not also 'I did *impetigo* thy *gratillity*,' from the French *gratiller*, to scratch a little?

We have been so fascinated by the fool's long coat that we have neglected to peep under it to see what he wore for breeches. Feste, as Maria's witty retort shows us, had on the great loose breeches called 'gaskins' or 'galligaskins,' held up by the laces called 'points':

Feste. I am resolv'd upon two points.
Maria. That if one breaks, the other will hold; or if both break, your gaskins fall.

That gaskins or loose breeches like Feste's were worn by other Tudor fools under the motley coat is clear from Lord North's expenditures on April Fools' Day, 1577, already noted. In addition to footing the bill for motley for hose and coat, Lord North also laid out six shillings and sixpence, for 'Foole Lackey . . . for motley for a pair of gascoins.' Huge galligaskins, though suitable for a fool, were evidently thought too exuberant a fashion for a sober student at Cambridge. In 1576 the Provost of Trinity censured one Stephen Lukes 'for his habit unbecoming a scholar. For he wore under his gown . . . a pair of galligastion hose. For this disguised apparel, so unmeet for a scholar, the provost punished him a week's commons.' [1]

---

[1] C. H. Cooper, *Annals of Cambridge* (1842–52), II. 346.

A further evidence of Feste's long coat has apparently quite escaped the notice of commentators. Sebastian, in trying to get rid of the Fool who persists in mistaking him for 'Cesario,' says, 'I prethee, foolish greeke, depart from me.' Not, be it noted, 'merry Greek,' which means mad-cap rascal, good fellow, or roistering boon companion, but *foolish Greek*. Why should a domestic fool remind Sebastian of a Greek? Possibly the Elizabethan meaning for *Greek*—'wily fellow, shifter, deceiver'—may also be present, but the primary explanation must lie in the close resemblance of the fool's long dress to the caftan or gaberdine of the Middle Easterners, of whom Thomas Heywood sings, 'And some like breech-lesse women go, The Rush, Turke, Jew, and Grecian.' [1] Among the theatrical costumes listed by Shakespeare's rivals, the Admiral's players, we find that the fool's gown, the Moor's flowing *aljuba*, and the Levantine and Scythian caftan were all classed as *coats*: 'Wm Someres cotte [i.e. a modern petticoat for Henry VIII's famous jester] . . . Mores cotte . . . Tamberlynes cotte.' [2] And when the notorious Jacobean pirate Captain Ward was reported to have 'turned Turk' in Barbary and to have adopted skirted Moorish *aljuba* and turban, the saying popularly put into his mouth was, 'I have a coat like a fool, And a head like an owl.' [3] Alongside Ward's owl we may place Florio's apt dictionary-definition of the bird called by the Italians *guffo*: 'An Owle called a Horne cout [coot] with feathers on each side of his head . . . Also a simple foole or grosse-pated gull, a ninnie-patch.'

[1] *A Challenge for Beauty* (1636), sig. H2^v.
[2] Chambers, *Eliz. Stage*, II. 168n., 178n.
[3] *Adventures by Sea of Edward Coxere*, ed. E. H. W. Meyerstein, p. 84.

The mental picture of the long Eastern caftan (which we should get from the term *Greek* applied to Feste) is supported by passages noticed by commentators in *King Lear*, when the 'mad' King looks at Edgar disguised as Tom o' Bedlam, *wrapped in a long blanket*. Plainly, Lear has some method in taking this outlandish skirted apparition for a 'Theban' or an 'Athenian,' and for his objection 'only, I do not like the fashion of your garments. You'll say they are Persian attire, but let them be chang'd.' Not long before the production of *Lear*, London had seen a Persian dress. 'In February 1600/1 Queen Elizabeth received an ambassador from Persia, Hassan Nabrech, accompanied by Sir Anthony Shirley. The Queen appeared in all her magnificance, and showed the Persian great honour.'[1] We also learn from a private letter, written in the summer following, that the Persian ambassador turned up at Rome, 'attended with Fifty persons in coates of cloth of Bodkin, being after the turckish maner longe with sleeves, one of which being heere in England is valued at fifty Poundes.'[2]

Having found additional evidence showing that both Touchstone and Feste wore the idiot's long motley coat on the stage, we now come to the last of Shakespeare's great trio, the 'sweet' Fool of Lear. He shows us the *material* of his costume by pointing to himself with the remark, 'the one in motley here.' As for the *form* of his dress, since we know that Lear's Fool (unlike the 'artificials' Touchstone and Feste) is presented as a true lackwit, a 'natural' or 'innocent,' called 'boy' and 'knave' by his master, he is also unquestionably garbed in the child-

[1] *C. S. P. Venice 1592–1600*, No. 958.
[2] John Cornwallis, Bodl. MS. Tanner 285, f. 10.

ish long coat or petticoat of the idiot. With his long-coated figure in mind, we now perceive to the full what the distracted Lear is imagining in the Hovel scene, when in wild fancy he is creating a special commission to try the criminal daughters arraigned in his mind's eye. Glancing about for judges, men of law, 'gentlemen of the long robe,' whom does he see ready at hand? To begin with, Edgar *in his long blanket* seems admirably suited to sit as the 'robéd man of justice.' This point has been noticed by commentators. But what of the other necessary judge, 'his yokefellow of equity'? Only now do we realize how aptly dressed is the Fool *in his long motley robe* to 'bench by his side.'

VI. WILL SOMMER IN MODERN
MOTLEY

WE have reviewed such a wealth of Elizabethan references to the long motley coat that when we look once more at the drawing of it in the Frontispiece, it now begins to seem familiar. Later in the present chapter the picture will be discussed in detail. But to forestall a possible misunderstanding, I must anticipate that discussion by pointing out one respect in which this drawing might mislead us. For though it does present a true picture of the costume of the Shakespearean Fool, which for our purpose is the essential, it does not show Will Sommer 'in his habit as he lived' back in the days of Henry VIII. As we shall see, the historical Will Sommer did not wear anything resembling the idiot's long motley coat common under Elizabeth and James. The picture is therefore only another example of the habitual Elizabethan anachronism of representing historical figures in modern dress.

The Elizabethans regarded Will Sommer as inseparable from his master, Bluff King Hal. Keeping this ever-present association of theirs in mind, we shall find it both interesting and profitable to consider the stage presentation of Shakespeare's play of *Henry VIII*.

On the last Tuesday in June, 1613, a crowded house at the Globe on the Bankside had gathered to see the King's Men introduce Shakespeare's *Henry VIII*, alternatively entitled *All is True*. Pomp and majesty, sumptuous costume, rich hangings: there was even matting on the stage-floor. No expense had been spared to grace the great and grim tragedies of Henry's absolutism. When all was ready for the start, on the trumpets' third sounding out paced a figure robed to the heels in black velvet and crowned with poet's bays, to make his three obeisances and to deliver the Prologue. This may very well have been the author, Shakespeare himself, in his last appearance on the stage.

At this point we find ourselves interrupted by a curious question raised by critics: was Shakespeare the author of *Henry VIII*? For a latter-day theory has attempted, on internal grounds of style exclusively, to deny most of this play to Shakespeare and to ascribe it to John Fletcher, or perhaps to Philip Massinger—authors whose names were never mentioned by any contemporary in connection with it. Professor Peter Alexander, however, after examining the conjectural grounds alleged for depriving Shakespeare of full authorship, is clearly right in rejecting the theory.[1] As Alexander says, the actor-editors John Heminges and Henry Cundall, the poet's intimate friends, included *Henry VIII* in their collection for the 1623 Folio as one of Shakespeare's plays 'absolute in their numbers, as he conceived them.' We have no grounds whatever for doubting either their knowledge or their integrity. Further, their testimony is supported by that of their contemporary, the distinguished man of letters Leonard Digges, stepson of Shakespeare's close friend Thomas Russell, who likewise writes from personal observation and knowledge of the poet's activities. In his alternative set of verses written

---

[1] See 'Conjectural History, or Shakespeare's *Henry VIII*,' *Essays and Studies Engl. Assoc.* XVI (1931), 85–120; also his *Shakespeare's Life and Art* (1939), 218–221.

for the Folio of 1623, Digges unhesitatingly declares
Shakespeare's independence of collaboration:

> ... for look through
> This whole book, thou shalt find he doth not borrow ...
> Nor begs he from each witty friend a scene
> To piece his acts with: all that he doth write
> Is pure his own—plot, language exquisite.

In modern times, however, Digges's last line has been
subjected to misinterpretation. For on the ground that
'Shakespeare borrowed most of his plots,' it has been
supposed that Leonard Digges didn't know what he was
talking about.[1] This judgment appears singularly ill-
considered. It assumes, quite unjustifiably, that Digges
used the word 'plot' in our narrow modern sense of 'the
framework of the fable.' On the contrary, by 'plot' he
almost certainly meant *planned theme* or *subject,* as the
term is used in *The Arte of English Poesie* (1589): 'Our
maker or Poet is ... first to devise his plat or subject,
then to fashion his poem.' A thoughtful criticism has in
modern times rediscovered the age-old truth that *character
is plot*; and Digges knew at least as well as we do that
Shakespeare's essential *subjects,* like those of the Greek
dramatists, are not the bare skeletons of old stories he
uses in common with all writers—what we call 'plots'—
but the *living themes as developed by his characters*; and
that these are his own. It is in this deep and significant
sense that Digges in his eulogy uses the term. He mentions no 'plots' whatever in our mechanical and superficial 'boy meets girl' sense of the word. What stirs him

---

[1] The mistake is repeated in Miss Marchette Chute's *Shakespeare
of London*, p. 292.

to enthusiasm is 'passions of Juliet and her Romeo,' 'Caesar,' 'Brutus and Cassius,' 'Honest Iago,' 'the jealous Moor,' 'Falstaff,' 'Hal, Poins,' 'Beatrice and Bene-dick,' 'Malvolio'—*characters* in action. In short, by say-ing 'all . . . —plot, language exquisite,' Digges means to embrace in two words Shakespeare's undeniable and un-matched originality, both of dramatic conception and of expression.

Returning to the matter of the authorship of *Henry VIII*, let us here also cling to common sense. Fletcher was alive when the Folio appeared. If he was indeed the author of most of this play, is it for a moment conceivable that the editors Heminges and Cundall, and their con-tributor Digges, would gratuitously court inevitable contradiction by publicly ascribing to Shakespeare every bit of work included in the volume? If we are ever tempted 'on stylistic grounds' to the presumption of thinking that we today can tell more precisely what Shakespeare was able to write, and did write, than his intimates could, we might take warning by a recent and salutary experience. Some lines of Elizabethan poetry—on grounds of style—were confidently ascribed by modern critics to Christopher Marlowe, *until* a discovery by Mr. John Crow demonstrated that they were in fact written by Gervase (Jervis) Markham.[1]

To come again to that afternoon in June, 1613, which saw the production of Shakespeare's new play at the Globe. We know that this was certainly the last perform-ance of any kind on those historic boards which had borne up his highest triumphs. For towards the close of the

---

[1] 'Marlowe yields to Jervis Markham,' by John Crow. *The Times Literary Supplement*, January 4, 1947.

first act, the unlucky flight of a smouldering wad from a cannon salute set fire to the thatched roof, and the playhouse burnt to the ground. The fiery fate impending was not to be foreseen by the Prologue. What its author did however foresee, and endeavour to forestall, was the audience's insistent demand for a Fool in this play. And their cry would not be for any random fool, either, but for a particular Fool: for King Harry's inseparable companion, Will Sommer.[1] A prince's fool, Will Sommer had been incontestably the prince of fools, and Englishmen cherished his memory fresh and green a half-century after his death. His merry but mordant and fearless wit, which for preference he shot at the overweening Cardinal Wolsey, made the delight of playgoers of the Elizabethan generations succeeding. When Shakespeare's rivals the Admiral's players put on *The Rising of Cardinal Wolsey*, Sommer was staged in modern dress, wearing a 'Wm Someres cotte,' the long motley of the Elizabethan idiot. A similar 'Will Sommer' cuts an indispensable figure in Samuel Rowley's piece on Henry VIII, performed before 1605 under the apt title, *When you see me, you know me*.

As they prepared to listen to Shakespeare's new *Henry VIII* on this day in June, there could therefore be no doubt of what 'the first and happiest hearers of the town'

---

[1] We have this name in two main forms, with and without a final *s*. In Sommer's lifetime it appears always without the *s*: The Wardrobe Accounts of the Royal Household give 'Sommar'; Ascham's *Toxophilus*, 'Somer'; Account of Funeral of Queen Mary, 'Somer'; Wilson, *Arte of Rhetorique*, 'Sommer'. Later writers often preserved the original form. Nashe gives both 'Summer' and 'Summers'; Gabriel Harvey (*Pierce's Supererogation*), 'Sommer'; Dekker (*Gull's Hornbook*), 'Sommer'; Florio (s.v. *Dabudà*), "Will-sommer'; Brathwait (*A Good Wife*), 'Sommer'; and Haryngton (notes on *Orlando Furioso*), 'Will Sommer.'

would expect and claim virtually as their due. Shakespeare in his Prologue nevertheless not only declined to oblige them, but rated them in these words for demanding Will Sommer:

> I come no more to make you laugh, Things now,
> That beare a Weighty, and a Serious Brow,
> Sad, high, and working, full of State and Woe:
> Such Noble Scœnes, as draw the Eye to flow
> We now present. Those that can Pitty, heere
> May (if they thinke it well) let fall a Teare,
> The Subject will deserve it. . . . Onely they
> That come to heare a Merry, Bawdy Play,
> A noyse of Targets: Or to see a Fellow
> In a long Motley Coate, garded with Yellow,
> Will be deceyv'd. For gentle Hearers, know,
> To ranke our chosen Truth with such a show
> As Foole, and Fight is, beside forfeyting
> Our owne Braines, and the Opinion that we bring
> To make that onely true, we now intend,
> Will leave us never an understanding Friend.

Most pregnant and persuasive. When it is put like that, who so foolish as to persist in clamour for Will Sommer? But if Shakespeare had but allowed them leisure to consider, some could have pointed out the shallowness of his specious reasons. In the first place, one might deny his major assumption. For, whatever they might look for in a piece by Rowley, people did not usually come to a history-play of Shakespeare's expecting a bawdy merriment loud with fool and fight. What is more, in his tragic *Hamlet*, which had certainly borne a weighty and a serious brow, had not the melancholy Prince not only summoned up the memory of a jester of infinite wit, but under the guise of an antic disposition actually played the bitter fool himself? For that matter his *King Lear* had been sad, high, and working, full of state and woe; yet he had been able to add to its terror the pity of the rarest 'natural' Fool of all. How then, Master Shakespeare? We know your unique power of heightening a tragedy with a fool. If, as you protest, All is True, why not a Will Sommer for your Henry? For in truth Will had lived as an ingrafted limb of King Harry's life.

Why not? The reason was simple but cogent. Robert Armin had retired from the stage. And as Shakespeare had begun to write fools' parts with *All's Well*, *As You Like It*, and *Twelfth Night* because in Armin he had found a great actor to play them, so now, with Armin gone, he would write no more in that kind. None but Armin could have presented for his *Henry VIII* a Will Sommer who would enhance the tragic mood. Better no Will Sommer at all.

If we inquire what costume the disappointed audience of 1613 would have expected to see on an actor portraying the deathless Will Sommer, we can answer in detail, for it is shown in several ways. First, in the Prologue by Shakespeare himself: 'a Fellow In a long Motley Coate, garded with Yellow.' Armin, too, told us in his *Foole upon Foole* of Sommer's 'best fooles coate' and cap; and in his *If you know not me*, Rowley made King Harry say to Sommer, 'Well *William*, I am beholding to ye. Ye shall have a new Coate and cap for this.' As we noted at the beginning of the chapter, however, the full ocular evidence of the Elizabethan and Jacobean idea of Will Sommer's appearance is supplied by our Frontispiece. This is an engraving by Francis Delaram, produced a few years after Shakespeare's *Henry VIII*, and entitled 'Will Sommers, Kinge Heneryes Jester.' Here he is seen modernized as the typical Elizabethan Fool in the long motley coat—the mixed colour indicated by small spots —adorned with two velvet guards at the hem. Of the loose-hanging extra pair of sleeves we shall hear in the sequel. Tucked into his knotted girdle is the child's or idiot's necessary 'muckender'—'a cleanly cloth thy moisture for to wipe'—mentioned in Fletcher's *The Captain* (3.1):

Jacomo.   Well, I will be your fool now ...
Fabritio.   We'll have a bib. .... And a fringed muckender hang at thy girdle.

On his head he wears a cap, with the feather which sometimes replaced the bell or the 'cock's comb' of red cloth.[1] His office in the royal household is marked not merely by the triple chain, but also by the letters H and R for *Henricus Rex* embroidered on the bosom of his coat.

That the usual *green* would be the hue of his motley is evident in a variety of ways. The Jacobean Richard Brathwait, as we have seen, spoke of 'white for *William*, and greene for *Sommer*.' Again, Will's bugle-horn implies the huntsman—'betokens summer's game'—and the Elizabethan going a-hunting 'apparelled him selfe in greene, and about his neck a Bugle.'[2] (The Fool's bugle recalls John Aubrey's note on the bugles carried by Tom o' Bedlams—'which when they came to an house for almes, they did wind: and they did putt the drink given them into this horn.' Here is a clear hint to the pro-

---

[1] 'It will become them as well as a peacocks fether a fooles cap.'— Thomas Wright, *The Passions of the Mind* (1604), 111.
[2] Gascoyne, *A Hundreth sundrie Floures* (ed. C. T. Prouty), 78.

ducer of *King Lear*. Edgar's professional wail, ' Poor
Tom, thy horn is dry,' is plainly the signal for his
sending a useful shudder through the audience with an
eldritch blast on his madman's bugle.) Finally, we know
that green was the traditional colour for summer livery
at Court, and the lines engraved at the foot of the print
play on *summer* and *Sommer*:

What though thou thinkst mee clad in strange attire?
Knowe I am suted to my owne deseire:
And yet the Characters describ'd vpon mee
May shewe thee, that a King bestow'd them on mee.

This Horne I have, betokens Sommers game;
Which sportiue tyme will bid thee reade my [name:]
All with my Nature well agreeing too,
As both the Name, and Tyme, and Ha[bit do.]

This punning on *Sommer* and *summer coat* throws unexpected light on an obscure passage in *Twelfth Night*.
We remember that when Maria prophesies that Feste will
be turned away for his truancy, he retorts, 'for turning
away, let summer beare it out.' Perhaps the most
plausible gloss of this has been G. L. Kittredge's: 'let
summer make it endurable.' Yet in Elizabethan idiom the
transitive verb *bear out* does not mean 'make endurable.'
It has three definite senses, (*a*) 'to countenance or to back
up'; (*b*) 'to carry in view,' as a staff of office, or an
admiral's lantern; or—as here—(*c*) 'to *withstand* or *keep
off*,' as 'armour which will beare out [withstand] the pistoll
shott,' 'they beare out [ward off] the blow,' 'that you may
better beare out [keep off] violence.' Feste, the professional corrupter of words, naturally regards turning
away as a shrewd blow of Fortune's. And what will

'bear it out' or withstand it? Why (pointing to his coat),
summer: his 'Sommer,' or Fool's green motley coat of
proof. 'For turning away, let Sommer ward it off.' Like
Will Sommer, Feste can 'bear out' and even dissipate
righteous anger with a jest.

The 'jests nominal' on *Summer* the season and *Sommer*
the famous fool, on *Will* the name and *will* (testament),
were also exploited by Thomas Nashe in his privately-
acted play entitled *Summers Last Will and Testament*.
And in the performance the long motley coat of the
Elizabethan fool or 'natural' inevitably appeared. We
read that an actor named Toy took the part of 'Will
Sommer.' For costume, Toy borrowed the dress of
'Ned,' the domestic fool of the house where the play was
put on. The directions for Toy's entrance to deliver the
prologue read: *Enter Will Summers in his fooles coate but
halfe on.* In preparing this prologue, Nashe had disarmingly satirized himself by including this passage for
'Will Sommer' to say: 'I, a foole by nature, and by arte,
do speake to you in the person of the Idiot our Play-
maker.' We note as a picturesque detail that Nashe
agrees with Armin that the historical Will Sommer was
tall, thin, and stooping. Armin described Sommer in his
book of fools as follows:

> Leane he was, hollow eyde as all report,
> And stoop he did too, yet in all the Court
> Few men were more belov'd then was this foole,
> Whose merry prate, kept with the King much rule.

For Nashe's performance, we read that Toy played
Sommer 'stooping in the back.' And in the course of the
play the character Harvest draws attention to Will's

height by calling him 'goodman Lundgis' or 'lungis'—a tall, gangling looby.

As the play moves on, Bacchus undertakes to make the protesting Will drink more than half a gallon (apparently to the health of a horned 'captain cuckold'), with the words, 'This Pupillonian in the fooles coate shall have a cast of martins [two 'black jacks' of a quart] & a whiffe [a draught]. To the health of Captaine *Rinocerotry* [horned beast]: looke to it, let him have weight and measure.' 'Pupillonian' is no doubt one of Nashe's Italianate coinages—*pupil*, baby or child, *pupillone*, great baby—affectionately applied to the tall fool in the child's long coat.

Sommer's loose-hanging second pair of sleeves (seen in the Frontispiece) are evidently what the Italians called *maniche di brodoni*, which Florio translates as 'a kind of hanging sleeves'—furnishing the wearer with 'four elbows.' These extra sleeves, we find, were a favourite distinguishing feature of the Elizabethan fool's coat; for they are familiarly spoken of in such phrases as, 'O fond foole, worthy to weare a coate with foure elbowes'[1] and 'like a fooles coat with foure elbowes.'[2] In Heywood's *The Captives*, also, the arrest of Mildewe, the he-bawd, gives rise to some quibbles upon both the 'guards' and the 'elbows' of the fool-and-bawd's coat:

Raphael. Frends guard him safe.
Clowne. We will see his fooles coate guarded, ey and re-
              guarded too from slipping out of our fingers.
Godfrey. . . . fower elbowes! elbowe him off all sydes,
              gentlemen.

---

[1] Thomas Deloney, *Gentle Craft*, Act 2.
[2] McKerrow's Nashe, III. 23.

Finally, in the familiar Procemium to his *Gull's Hornbook*, Dekker declares that the 'motley is bought, and a coat with foure elbowes for any one that will weare it is put to making.' When they are convinced of their folly, Dekker believes, all sorts of simpletons 'will be glad to fit themselves in Will Sommer his wardrobe.' Although Deloney, on bringing the celebrated Will into his *Jack of Newberie*, does not mention the long coat, nevertheless like his fellow-writers he insists upon motley, presenting Sommer cracking jests with the maids in 'a motley Jerken' and 'motly hosen.'

At this point we may bring in the evidence (mentioned at the beginning of the chapter) to prove that for the actual Will Sommer of history garments of motley as well as long coats 'with four elbows,' as shown in the Frontispiece, were anachronistic inventions of the Elizabethans, to suit with their contemporary usage for domestic fools. An examination of the Wardrobe Accounts of Henry VIII discloses no motley whatever among the various garments actually issued to the King's genial Fool. In fact it is clear that Will Sommer was dressed very much like other minor officers of the royal household. Certainly he was not garbed fantastically to mark him out or set him off as a Fool, either in a petticoat or in some parti-coloured style borrowed from the century preceding.

Though we do find Sommer occasionally receiving gowns of blue damask, blue satin, or green figured velvet for sumptuous wear, his customary and common livery was the usual Tudor hooded knee-length 'Coate of grene cloth'—plain, or guarded with green velvet—like that issued to Henry's officers of the Robes, and to all the grooms of the Privy Chamber. This indeed is the very

HENRY VIII AND WILL SOMMER

A miniature in Henry VIII's own manuscript Psalter.
(B.M. MS. Royal 2A XVI, f. 63v.)

thing Will had on when he was painted with the King on one of the pages of Henry's own manuscript Psalter, preserved in the British Museum (MS. Royal 2A XVI, f. 63ᵛ). In this miniature we see that, over a white shirt stitched with black, Will wears the common hooded knee-length coat of his day, made of green cloth—cut full in body, skirt, and sleeves—and guarded or trimmed with a band of green velvet. Another painting, at Hampton Court, shows him in a similar knee-length coat, but of black, with red striping.[1]

In sum, nowhere during Will Sommer's lifetime do we hear of his wearing anything resembling the long coat of the idiot, double or hanging sleeves, or motley cloth. But in the succeeding age of Shakespeare, people were not curious about historical accuracy in matters of costume. If they were content with Prince Hamlet and King Henry V in Elizabethan dress, why should they have Will Sommer in anything but their familiar and modern idiot's coat of motley?

---

[1] 'Henry VIII and Family, School of Holbein.' Hampton Court Palace, No. H.5.

VII. ROBERT ARMIN, SHAKESPEARE'S
FOOL

WE cannot remind ourselves too often that Shakespeare was an actor. His incomparable eye for the significant and striking in human character was particularly trained upon what would prove effective on the stage. His dramatic characters were specifically devised for himself and his intimates to represent. Such a genius as his would not only prize peculiar mimetic powers in a fellow-player gifted with an 'experiencing nature,' but also exploit them to the full.

It has long been recognized that this is in fact what Shakespeare did when about 1599 he made the low-comedy clowning and *compère* turns of Kempe and Cowley, his leading comics of the 1590's, give way to the originality and high-comedy wit of the new and distinctive line of sagacious fools he introduced with Robert Armin. But both Shakespeare and Armin had their work cut out for them. It must have taken labour as well as their combined genius to develop in the 'general' a taste for high comedy, and to capture for the new witty and learned Fool the popularity which had long been the undisputed monopoly of the Clown. (The earlier 'Vice' had been a figure of crude Punch-like fun, belabouring the Devil with a wooden dagger, and riding off the stage on the Devil's back.)

Of Armin's predecessor the great clown Dick Tarlton it could justly be said, 'of all the Jesters in the lande he bore the praise awaie.' The chronicler Stow set it down

84

that Tarlton, 'for a wondrous plentiful, pleasant, and extemporall wit . . . was the wonder of his time.' His death in 1588 cast a cloud over the nation. Spenser's Thalia, as we have seen, lamented him as one

> *With whom all joy and jolly meriment*
> *Is also deaded, and in dolour drent.*

Tarlton's reigning humour had been always identified with the rustic 'uplandish man' or *clown*. His pre-eminence had therefore established a firm convention that the funny man in a play is naturally and inevitably a rustic or clown, appearing in russet jerkin and breeches, country boots, and buttoned cap. The humour of the character was drawn out of the unfailing well of the countryman's coarseness, his self-satisfaction, his vivid mother-wit, his craft in 'lying at catch' under a feigned stupidity, and his pagan mistaking of the language of the cultivated.

Legend has it that long before Armin joined Shakespeare's company Tarlton had taken such appreciative notice of the youth's brilliant comic gifts as to prophesy that 'without all paraquestions' he 'should enjoy my clownes sute after me.' Certainly Armin's subsequently published works showed skill in facile riming, an art which Tarlton used to exhibit extempore on the stage. As early as 1592 Armin could be included with Thomas Deloney and Philip Stubbes in the list of popular pamphleteers. Nashe mentions him as a 'son' of the leading balladeer William Elderton. Yet on coming about 1599 into his own as a leading player in Shakespeare's company, this new comic star showed judgment as well as courage in electing to wear not Tarlton's clown's suit, but the fool's coat: that is, not the rustic's russet, but the idiot's long coat of motley.

It was high time for a new departure. In the 1590's, the clown had flourished and luxuriated to the point of proving noxious to the drama. Tarlton had been a genius, but his thronging imitators could imitate no more than his costume, his tricks, his mannerisms. The 'clown's' tremendous vogue with the grosser element, which Prince Hamlet called the 'unskilful' or 'barren,' and the resulting crude impropriety of lugging rustic buffoons into scenes where they could have no possible place, elicited sharp satire in the Cambridge students' *Parnassus* play:

> *Enter* Dromo, *drawing a clown in with a rope.*
> *Clowne.* What now? thrust a man into the common-
> wealth whether he will or noe? what the divell
> should I doe here?
> *Dromo.* Why what an ass art thou! dost thou not knowe
> a play cannot be without a clowne? Clownes
> have bene thrust into playes by head and
> shoulders ever since Kempe could make a
> scurvey face; and therefore reason thou
> shouldst be drawne in with a cart-rope.

Sir Philip Sidney in his *Apologie for Poetrie* had reprehended the preposterous dramatic practice of mixing yokels and royalty. Whetstone in 1578 censured it likewise: 'Many times (to make mirthe) they make a Clowne companion with a Kinge.' And the satirist Joseph Hall (1591) condemned the crudeness with which such a low grimacing swain was often foisted into a scene of tragedy to shatter a mood that might prove possibly too much for an overstrained audience's self-control:

Now, least such frightfull showes of Fortunes fall,
And bloody Tyrants rage, should chance appall
The dead stroke audience, mids the silent rout
Comes leaping in a selfe-misforméd lout,
And laughes, and grins, and frames his Mimik face,
And justles straight into the princes place.
Then doth the Theatre Eccho all aloud,
With gladsome noyse of that applauding croud,
A goodly hoch-poch, *when vile* Russettings
Are match't with monarchs, and with mighty kings.

The clown in the midst may mar all. Shakespeare the playwright had more cause than Hall the satirist to apprehend damage from a spoiled and arrogant clown. Hamlet's strictures to the players on the abuse are cogent. But we know that within proper bounds Shakespeare had delighted to extract the quintessence of clownish talent from his fellows Kempe and Cowley. In *Much Ado* Dogberry and Verges, as R. B. McKerrow pointed out, 'were so life-like because they were not merely a constable and a watchman in the abstract, but actually Kempe and Cowley, whose every accent and gesture Shakespeare must have known, playing a constable and a watchman.' He was to do the same thing with the parts he wrote specifically for Armin, who also inherited Dogberry, though, we must believe, with a difference. As for Kempe and Cowley, however free this inimitable pair may have felt to improve the ordinary play with gags and 'business,' the roles lovingly fitted to them in *Much Ado* could hardly have tempted them to speak more than was set down.

Few institutions can be found more conservative than the theatre. Shakespeare's and Armin's introduction of the high-comedy professional Fool in long motley coat

—a character developed from domestic jesters in real life —in the place of the old favourite russet serving-man Clown was probably both more gradual and more judicious than we have realized. They were faced with the necessity of weaning their public little by little from its fanatic addiction to the Tarlton–Kempe–Cowley convention. A significant progression in the treatment of the role can be traced in the comedies *All's Well*, *As You Like It*, and *Twelfth Night*, in that order; and this development provides one argument for placing *All's Well* chronologically first.

In *All's Well*, to begin with, the jester Lavatch is made to divide the comic honours with the braggart Parolles. Lavatch's importance as titular Clown is thus deliberately reduced. What is more, he retains clown-like duties as a serving creature, and by his own account is the familiar 'woodland fellow' or rustic, longing to go the way of the world with the woman Isbel. In these characteristics he appears of a piece with the long-established Clown. But new qualities have begun to show themselves. In the text we find him repeatedly called *fool* or *knave* (that is, rascal, boy), but never *clown*; and to the fool's privilege of jesting is joined more than a suggestion of the fool's punishment for 'going too far'; for the bell involved the whip. The Countess's father had encouraged Lavatch to play the jester. And now, as though to put the rustic behind him, and to mount the first step on the stair to high comedy, Lavatch proceeds to court, is addressed as 'Monsieur,' and loses his taste for the Isbels of the country. His humble name—whose spelling shows it to be not the female-bovine *La Vache* but the scullion's *Lavages* (Ital. *Laváccio*), meaning Dishwater, Hogswash,

Swillings, or Draff, recalling Potpan of the black guard in *Romeo and Juliet*—stands in pointed contrast with the courtly accomplishments which begin to fit him for higher things. His galloping wit easily tramples Parolles, his songs are pleasant and full of fine conceits, his variations of 'O Lord, sir!' inimitable, and his polished tongue ingeniously sharp: a shrewd knave, and an 'unhappy,' or mischievous. In Lavatch the rustic serving-man Clown has not yet dropped out of sight, but with him Shakespeare and Armin have unmistakably begun to bring in the Fool.

As You Like It marks a further advance. In the character of the fool-and-knave Lavatch, Armin had stopped short of assuming the idiot guise and foolish garb. As Touchstone, however, posing as 'Nature's natural,' he is from the start inseparable from the long motley coat. The mixed greenish uniform of imbecility covers the foibles-hunter like a stalking-horse, under which his wit takes fatal aim. The long dress has another advantage over the curtal or bobtailed suit of the rustic and the serving-man: it resembles a worthy gentleman's surtout or gown sufficiently to make him 'Master Touchstone' to the shepherd Corin, a 'motley gentleman' to the ironic Jaques, and to the lowly William one to be off-capped to and sirred. These indications alone make it evident that Touchstone did not wear the antic parti-coloured hood, jerkin, and long hose of the medieval jester. To the Elizabethan eye that would have been a bizarre fancy-dress, in which even the most untravelled hind of Arden's backwoods could never mistake him for a gentleman. A passage from Armin's *Foole upon Foole* provides a fascinating parallel to Touchstone's being taken for a dignitary *because of his long coat*. Here Armin,

anachronistically picturing Will Sommer in the Elizabethan idiot's long coat, relates, 'as *Will* past by [the poor
people] saluted him, taking him for a worthy personage,
which pleased him.' It may well have been on a suggestion of this from Armin that Shakespeare added the Will
Sommer stroke to Touchstone.

Yet in Touchstone the characteristic Clown remains
more than a vestige, lending a faint air of plausibility to
the conservative stage-directions and speech-prefixes, in
which his designation throughout is persistently *Clown*.
Artificial Fool, scholar, experienced courtier though he is,
yet something of the old clown still clings. Lady Rosalind twits him with being the countryman's cousin, and
calls him 'clownish fool.' Though he himself would like
to pass for an urbane Ovid diselemented among the Goths
(or Gotes), the goats of Arden irresistibly rouse in him
firmly-suppressed memories of his rural origin. The over-
emphasis of his condescension to the shepherds betrays
him further; his recollections of Jane Smile are redolent
of the cowshed, and in the end his dubious wedding with
Audrey links him with the 'country copulatives.'

Not until we enter the Lady Olivia's courtly household
in *Twelfth Night* do we meet, in Feste, the Fool refined of
all clownish alloy. To be sure, the bigoted prompt-book
continues to repeat the now meaningless speech-prefix
Clown, but the text, both in letter and in spirit, is free of it.
The artificial Fool has at length shaken off all rustic
humour and memories bucolic. For us Feste in the
idiot's motley robe of privilege stands as the quintes-
sential high-comedy jester, the triumph of Shakespeare
and Armin in this kind. His wit is courtly, his admirable
fooling scholarly, his singing exquisite. The delight of

wise foolery is his whole spring of being. Set beside the brain of Feste, the little wit of Aguecheek shrinks further into imbecility.

'I have read in a booke, that to play the foole wisely, is high wisdome,' says Jonson's Albius in *The Poetaster*, echoing a Renaissance commonplace. Shakespeare indeed goes out of his way to press home to the audience's mind the value of this highly exacting and ticklish role. He gives Viola a reflective verse-soliloquy on Feste which carries the authority of a Chorus:

> This fellow's wise enough to play the fool,
> And to do that well craves a kind of wit:
> He must observe their mood on whom he jests,
> The quality of persons, and the time;
> Not, like the haggard, check at every feather
> That comes before his eye. This is a practice
> As full of labour as a wise man's art.

The justice of this high appreciation became widely recognized. In Jonson's *Staple of Newes* Gossip Tattle declared, 'The Foole is the finest man i' the company, they say, and has all the wit.' King and Fool came to be reckoned the leading dramatic roles, and the ironical Donald Lupton, writing on 'Playhouses' in 1632, agreed that in the players' troupe 'most commonly the wisest man is the fool.' Much later, in *The Woman Captain* of 1680, Thomas Shadwell's Fool maintained flatly that 'Shakespeare's fools had more wit than any of the wits and critics nowadays': that is, than the logical and rules-ridden critic Thomas Rymer and his like. To our minds today this is a truism; but in 1680 to set the mental power of Shakespeare's fools above the heavy brains of Restoration 'intellectuals' took some courage.

As ruler of the revels in *Twelfth Night,* that most spirited, gay, and graceful of courtly comedies, Feste remains for us the Jester supreme. The wise wit and charm of the artificial Fool could hardly mount higher. But close on the heels of this triumph at Court Shakespeare turned to tragedy, for his greatest work, *Hamlet.* And here a specious question might be raised. Why, it might be asked, has the Fool—now brought to such perfection by Shakespeare and Armin—not been employed with a difference in the tragedy of *Hamlet?* At first glance Shakespeare seems here to have abandoned the ground gained, retreated into the old *compère* convention of the Clown, dwindled from the wit of Feste into the chop-logic of a couple of grave-digging swains.

More than once, however, it has been pointed out that the question is mistaken. The Fool has not really been omitted. For does not the 'transformed' Prince himself provide a full feast of the word-corrupting, the privileged mockery, the traditionally ribald and railing wit, the bitter gibes as amusing as they are insolent, and the lightning-rod nonsense to distract anger, of a brilliant 'natural,' or fool with wits diseased? Clearly, the Prince doubles as Fool. Shakespeare has here subtilized and enriched with new method the madness essential to the old Hamlet story. In the ancient savage tale the crafty avenger must play the lunatic to save his own life—in the manner of David, who at the court of the King of Gath 'changed his behaviour before them, and feigned himself mad in their hands, and scrabbled on the doors of the gate.' In Shakespeare, Hamlet's knavish-mad buffoonery is similarly successful. They 'fool' him to the top of his bent.

Centring our attention on the essential purpose of this

seemingly bizarre feature of the play, it will pay us to follow the progress of the 'transformed' Hamlet a little farther. Playing the lunatic fool, or, as he calls it, 'being idle,' serves his purpose well. It covers him through his testing and catching of his uncle's guilty conscience in the dramatic *Mousetrap*, to his swift extermination of the supposed Claudius like a rat in his mother's closet. But the death of Polonius is the turning-point. Already warned by the springing of *The Mousetrap*, the King takes the alarm. Plainly, for Claudius it is now kill or be killed. The dangerous fool is 'most immediate' to his throne, and is not a tool like Laertes to be put off by persuasive talk. Mocking the divinity that doth hedge a king, Hamlet has got within his hollow crown, and means Death—as surely and sardonically as in the picture drawn by Shakespeare's Richard II:

> . . . there the antic sits,
> Scoffing his state, and grinning at his pomp,
> Allowing him a breath, a little scene,
> To monarchize, be fear'd . . .

Yet with all his eloquence and courage, Claudius lacks Hamlet's will-power and resolution in action. He dares not kill the deadly seeming-lunatic prince himself—not even with his favourite concealed weapon of poison—but secretly delegates the murder to the far-away King of England. This irresolution and delay in Claudius, for which he naturally gives himself the best of reasons—to keep his ill-won Queen—, in the end proves fatal to him.

A curious misconception has in modern times grown up round Hamlet's behaviour as an antic or mad Fool. His histrionic efforts to convince Ophelia of his madness, while thoroughly successful with her, have been strangely treated of late. More than one latter-day critic, ignoring the old tradition of histrionic ribaldry, and following a fashion now happily growing stale, has been led into Freudian and neurological musings by what he imagines to be Hamlet's 'cruel obscenities' addressed to Ophelia. Such fancies, which neglect Lamb's penetrating analysis of this unmeant bitterness, have produced heavy speculation about 'sex-nausea,' and not a little gratuitous and anguished pity for Ophelia. But is not the topic quite irrelevant both to Shakespeare and to the Elizabethan conception of the characters? The plain points to be held firmly in mind in considering the role which Hamlet has assumed are two: first, that ribaldry from an 'antic' or mad fool was older than history, always expected (see Lear's Fool), and if witty was commonly found amusing—'your best fool is your broad railing fool'; and second, that in her scene with 'mad' Hamlet, Ophelia is clearly distressed not by his wild satire on womankind, but by the proof it provides that his fine mind has cracked: that Hamlet 'from himself is ta'en away.' In the scene at *The Mousetrap* she humours his supposed distraction, and by his first loose sallies is so little shocked as to comment, 'You are merry, my lord.' And when his talk grows too broad, she tells him he's naughty. Her response to his later bawdy suggestion is merely to applaud the wit while disapproving the sentiment: 'Still better, and worse.'

His antic disposition for the moment laid aside, Hamlet treats us to his views—evidently shared by his creator—both of overweening stage clowns and of witty court jesters. In talking with the players, he issues some sharp advice to the Clown against taking too much on himself and spoiling the play. As for the clever artificial Fool or

Jester, in the graveyard scene a mouldering skull calls up delighted memories of the brilliant Yorick—dead and gone with the best of men, King Hamlet—which serve to lay bare by contrast the retrograde present under the hard-drinking Claudius. In the good old days, there had been a rare fellow of infinite jest, whose flashes of merriment were wont to set the table on a roar. Far otherwise in the degenerate present. Now, on this sterile promontory in the midst of death, no higher entertainment is to be had than the graveyard chop-logic of a pair of clownish delvers.

It was of course not Armin but Burbage who undertook 'young Hamlet,' that most subtle and difficult of roles, with its quick shifts into an antic disposition. Thus obliged to steal Armin's thunder, Burbage may well have profited not merely from observation, but also from the personal coaching of the expert Armin, who could 'give him intelligence for his action.' For there is the closest likeness between the method of Lear's 'motley innocent' in masking his keen thrusts, and that of the antic Hamlet. Everyone recalls the Fool's daring sallies in support of his King, as thus:

> '*The hedge-sparrow fed the cuckoo so long*
> *That it had it head bit off by it young.*
> So out went the candle, and we were left darkling.'

Also, 'May not an ass [fool] know when the cart draws the horse? Whoop, Jug, I love thee!' A shrewd cut of Hamlet's is similarly covered by a flight into the ridiculous:

> 'The body (*Polonius*) is with the King (*is with Old Hamlet among the dead*), but the King (*Claudius*) is not

with the body (*is not yet killed*). The King is a thing
... of nothing (*of naught, wicked*). Bring me to him.
Hide fox and all after!' [*Runs out.*]

We see that Burbage's 'mad' fooling in the character of
Hamlet looks forward to Armin's role in *Lear*. And in
Lear tragic poignancy is sharpened by the bold stroke
of turning from make-believe to realism. For in place of
the philosopher playing the wit-crazed fool, this more
universal tragedy presents the true idiot-fool or 'natural'
urging sharp truths in a vain effort to make his beloved
master 'see better.' Masked as bitter jests, their gnomic
wisdom is like that of a Greek chorus.

To understand Lear's Fool we should have a clear idea
of the peculiar position of the 'natural' in the mind of
Shakespeare's audience. Distinction between the born
fool and the artificial (who for advantage chose to adopt
the idiot's long motley coat) was of course fundamental, and commonly understood. An 'artificial' was a
thoroughly sane and clever hireling, a chargeable servant
or retainer, who assumed the character of jester-idiot in a
household for pay. The most conspicuous 'naturals,' on
the other hand, were idiot wards to whom their masters
stood as guardians, having begged or bought the wardship of the King. We shall enlarge on this presently.
The 'naturals,' being persons of property, were therefore
sources of income far beyond their expense, since the
guardian enjoyed the 'natural's' revenue and the use of his
property during life. 'Naturals' of this kind consequently
found themselves well cared for, their health and life
safeguarded. We may be sure that some of them were
lucid enough to realize both their situation and their
value, as the following anecdote implies:

A rich landed foole whom a Courtier had beggd & caryed about to waite on him, coming with his Master to a gentlemans house where the picture of a foole was wrought in a fayre suit of Arras, cutt the picture out with a penknife, & being chidden for so doeing, You have more cause, said he, to thanke me, for if my Master had seen the picture of the foole he would have beggd the hangings of the King as he did my lands.[1]

'To beg a man for a fool' was, then, to apply to the sovereign through the Court of Wards for a grant of the wardship: for by the statute 'the King shall have the lands of an Ideot or naturall Fool, taking the profits during his Life . . . and after his Death shall render the Lands to the right heir. . . . And the King shall also have the Custody of the Body, Goods, and Chattels of an Ideot.' This was however the King's prerogative only if the idiot was a true 'natural,' that is, born a fool; not if he were found to have lost his wits by chance or misfortune. And it was held axiomatic that 'to be a fool born is a disease incurable.' In executing the writ *of inquiring into or examining an idiot*, a favourite test of a right mind was 'numbering,' or counting up to ten. (This we find echoed by the Jailer's distracted Daughter in *The Two Noble Kinsmen*: 'You are a foole: tell ten. I have pozd him.') Among courtiers the custom of begging the wardship of an idiot as a ready means of adding to one's income was freely practised. 'Now Courtiers use to begge for fooles All such as cannot number,' sings Davys in his *Hymnes to Astrœa*; and Marston's Maquerelle regards breach of promise as a thing 'as common as *naturall* to a Courtier.' Ned Planet, in *Jack Drum's Entertainment*, confesses 'I have followed

---

[1] B.M. MS. Sloane 517, f. 33.

97

Ordinaries [eating-houses] this twelvemonth, onely to finde a Foole that had landes ... that I might beg him. *John*, be my Warde *John*, faith Ile give thee two Coates a yeere and be my Foole.' The custom still flourished under Charles II, for the monarch was heard to muse, 'It is very strange that every one of my friends keeps a tame knave.'

Naturally it was all to the good if the propertied idiot proved to be an interesting character, or had an amusing vein of folly. I find diverting illustration of the obtaining of such a ward, contained in some passages of a suit in the Court of Requests, 1613, between two Yorkshire gentlemen, Alexander Hartley (an attorney) and Sir Robert Dyneley. In his complaint, Hartley said that Sir Robert, being 'very desyrous to intertayn into his howse an Idiott or foole naturall to recreat him withall and to make him sporte,' through a kinsman found out one Robert Wheatley, 'a very naturall Foole and an Idiot, and yet of such pleasant disposition and Carriage, as the said Sir Robert Dyneley having once gott the sight of him and heard his pleasant disposition, and therewithall understanding that the said Idiot had a portion of one hundreth and thirtie powndes ... became so much the more desyrous of him the said Idiott.' Further, when the wardship was obtained, Sir Robert took the idiot 'into his tuition and service And made him apparell fitt for him, That is to say, a long cote, a fantasticall Cap and such like attyre the better to solace and make sporte for the saide Sir Roberte.' [1]

Elsewhere in Elizabethan writing we find a more serious tone. For example, the preacher points out that 'God's

---

[1] P.R.O. Req. 2/443.

fools' should make us thankful for the gift of an inborn knowledge of right and wrong withheld from them: '. . . the Lord in every place gives us monitors to put us in minde of this duetie: as we see in many borne fooles: the common use or abuse of whom, is ordinarily this: to make them our jesting stockes and subject of mirth. It were an holy use of them, if we kept them as spectacles of Gods mercy to us, with whom it hath pleased God to deale more mercifully in this behalfe.' [1] The layman's view was similar, when he wrote of 'the delight which we commonly take in innocents, which were kept in auncient times by great men, partly for spectacles of horror and humility; partly for charity.' [2] Such passages as these point significantly to the moral of the 'natural' in the tragedy of *Lear*. First, the King's treatment of the Fool shows his fundamental charity. Later, when Lear's sufferings bring him to the brink of madness, the Fool's presence is a continual reminder of God's mercy to him in the past, and a 'spectacle of humility.'

Glimpses such as these show us the Elizabethans accustomed to seeing a variety of peculiar defective mentalities treated as children and as accepted members of the family. Those found 'pleasant,' or capable of comment on the passing scene, were encouraged in uttering the shrewd, the unexpected, the indiscreet, the bizarre. Their extra-rational preoccupations could point a moral as well as amuse. The contemporary Edward Daunce described Queen Elizabeth's own 'phantasime' named Monarcho. He was an Italian, and perhaps called 'monarch' because of his fixed idea—in the manner of the

---

[1] William Sclater, *A Key to the Key of Scripture* (1611), sig. H4.
[2] Joseph Wybarne, *The New Age of Old Names* (1609), 54.

insatiable Philip of Spain—that all the ships sailing in and out of London River belonged to him. In stormy weather his tortured anxiety for the safety of his merchant navy was as enthralling as it was pitiful to see. A poor mad creature known as Mother Chicken, 'which did resort to the court,' was also a familiar figure about town, like Blue John of the Hospital.

For Shakespeare's audience it is plain that Lear's Fool, in his unobtrusive and humble robe of motley, was far from cutting any outlandish figure, or bringing in an atmosphere of romance or long-ago. He belonged to the contemporary scene, and his introduction by Shakespeare into tragedy was therefore a step towards realism, and away from what Sir Philip Sidney had reprobated as that gross absurdity of 'mingling Kings and Clownes,' of thrusting in crude rustic 'Clownes, by head and shoulders, to play a part in majesticall matters, with neither decencie nor discretion.' Rustics were not companions of kings, and were therefore out of place in tragedy. Fools or 'naturals,' on the other hand, belonged in the circles of high life, and might properly appear in 'majestical matters.' This consideration should have its weight in modern production and criticism, together with the realization, long overdue, that *motley* was not at all a gaudy parti-colour, but an undemonstrative vesture of humility.

It is one thing to be familiar with the appearance of 'naturals,' quite another, however, to be a connoisseur or an expert in their mysterious minds; and in this respect Robert Armin had a store of unique experience available to Shakespeare. His book *Foole upon Foole* testifies to his close study of the strange qualities and doings of certain actual living 'naturals.' If any player breathed who could explore with Shakespeare the shadows and fitful flashes of the borderland of insanity, that player was Armin. His writings reveal his keen observation as kindly, and his heart as Christian. Never for a moment did he forget that 'God's fools' stand under a special protection, and are at times granted an insight denied to the merely sane. With Armin at hand, Shakespeare could dare to present the tortured Lear hounded by unnatural and bemadding sorrow to the verge of the abyss, held back by one who knew its deeps. 'Fools cure not mad folks' is a true saying. Yet though pining for the loss of Cordelia, the Fool remained devoted to the King, and laboured to 'outjest his heart-struck injuries.' Instinct and love urged him from the beginning to rouse Lear to learn to know himself before the stunning blows of his ungrateful daughters' cruelty should drive reason from its seat. Few passages in all tragedy are more poignant than this crossing of folly in the wisdom of Lear by wisdom in the folly of the Fool. We may suspect that more is suggested here than anyone has grasped since Shakespeare and Armin first created the characters for the stage.

The fellow-player upon whom Shakespeare could confidently make such demands merits far more attention than he has ever received. When we think about Armin, we realize that he is the only colleague of Shakespeare's with whom we can really grow acquainted. For he was author as well as actor. The book is the man, and Armin's personality shines through the pages both of his *Foole upon Foole* (1600) and his subsequent comedy of *The Two Maids of More-clacke*. The first of these was published shortly after he had joined Shakespeare's company. Nothing could be keener or livelier, and at the same time more

ROBERT ARMIN IN THE ROLE
OF BLUE JOHN

sound, charitable, and sympathetic than his observation
of the varieties of human character. His zest for life is
infectious: no wonder the genius of Tarlton saw in him a
worthy successor. He has the sure human touch. His
extraordinary versatility is witnessed to by the different
parts he assumed in his own comedy, *The Two Maids*.
Here is no mere feat of 'doubling,' but one of 'quadrup-
ling.' The play's chief attraction, and the chief interest of
its author, lies in its realistic presentation of the well-
known contemporary London 'natural,' the aged child or
veteran infant protégé of Christ's Hospital, called Blue
John. In *Foole upon Foole* Armin had versified his

'description of John of the Hospitall, a very foole,' in these terms:

> What need description in so plaine a creature,
> Knowne to all London since he liv'd so late:
> And then to erre what folly can be greater,
> When every boy knew him in his estate.
>
> *John* was a very foole that all men knowes,
> Flat cap, blew coate, and Ickorne by his side:
> A nurse to tend him, to put on his cloathes,
> Yet was a man of olde yeares when he dy'd.
>
> Two staring eyes, a black beard and his head
> Lay on his shoulder still, as sicke and sad:
> And till the very time that he was dead,
> He halted with the dearest friend he had.[1]
>
> Then *vale John*, thee and thy Lady too,
> For lacke of wit both bore away the bell:
> Therefore the most that I can say or doe,
> To thee or her, is to say fooles farewell.

At various times in the performance of his *Two Maids*, Armin played four different parts: first, that of Blue John; then that of the Clown, or rather Fool, Tutch. He also appeared as Tutch disguised as Blue John, and finally, as Tutch impersonating a Welsh knight.

It is obvious that he was a gifted 'character' actor, and one who by his warm personality would instantly win the audience to his side. He could be relied on by Shake-

---

[1] Armin's neat pun here is obscure to modern ears. His two senses seem to be 'limped with his nurse' and 'paltered or shuffled with his best friend.' For this second sense the *O.E.D.* quotes Queen Elizabeth: 'I cannot halt with you so much as to denye that I have seen such evident shewes of your contrarious dealings.'

speare to body forth those delicate roles whose interpretation can make or mar a performance. A suggestion which strikes me as most plausible is that Armin, as Shakespeare's leading comic actor, probably played Menenius, the beloved friend whom Coriolanus called 'father': that warmly human old patrician whose practical wisdom is lighted by a humour which, if the part be truly realized, makes him irresistible. We remember that the demagogues, who had called him 'giber' or scoffer, in the end come begging to him as their last hope of averting the avenger's wrath. And when he makes his appeal to Coriolanus only to be rejected heart-broken, the enemy Volscian guards who first took him for a 'decay'd dotant' find him noble. In this austere and painful study of the devastating effects of an inculcated virtue and pride carried to a logical extreme, Menenius provides the saving touch of human kindness.

And what of Armin in *Hamlet*, where, as we have recalled, Burbage as the melancholy Prince pre-empts the part of the bitter Fool? Professor Baldwin is doubtless correct in conjecturing that Armin found a role in the First Gravedigger, but I am tempted to think that as leading comedian Armin may have doubled as Polonius. We recognize Polonius as a character-part of great importance and delicacy, one not to be mocked or burlesqued without irreparable loss. Polonius shares with Menenius the extrovert's complete self-confidence, as well as the sure human touch in establishing close relations with all the world—talents which were unmistakably the birthright of Armin. The pathos implicit in both these humorous characters was peculiarly suited to Armin's genius.

A player so gifted as to be able to body forth in out-ward reality for Shakespeare conceptions such as Dog-berry, Lavatch, Touchstone, Feste, Lear's Fool, and possibly Menenius and Polonius among others, earns our everlasting gratitude. Anything we can learn or deduce about this indispensable colleague of Shakespeare's will be of price. We now turn to the search for more facts about Armin's origin and career, and we shall see that almost every new-found detail throws some kind of interesting light.

It has long been known that Armin was said to have been apprenticed to a goldsmith,[1] and a quarter of a century ago Professor E. M. Denkinger began the work of establishing Armin's biography more precisely.[2] In the books of the Goldsmiths' Company of London she traced the signed entry of his apprenticeship, dated 1581,[3] which we may paraphrase as follows: 'I, Robart Armin, son of John Armyn, tailor, of Lynn, Norfolk, do put myself apprentice to John Lonyson, goldsmith, of London, for eleven years from October 13, 1581. By me Robart Armin.' Thus we find that Robin Armin (like the more famous author Robin Greene, who called Shakespeare an 'upstart crow') came from Norfolk in East Anglia, and that his father had been a tailor in King's Lynn. And since we know that terms of apprenticeship were commonly

---

[1] We have recently added Shakespeare's trustee Thomas Savage, who hailed from West Lancashire, as another goldsmith-friend of the poet's.

[2] *Publ. Mod. Lang. Association*, XLI (1926).

[3] 'Memorandum that I Robart Armin ye sonne of John Armyn of Lynn in the county of Norff. taylor do put myself prentys vnto John Lowyson [rectè Lonyson] Sitizen and goldsmythe of London for the terme of xj yeares beginning at the xiij^th day of October in Anno 1581 By me Robart Armin.'

calculated to end at the age of twenty-four, this evidence would place our actor's birth about 1568, or four years after Shakespeare's. (As for John Lonyson, Armin's goldsmith-master, we shall return to him.)

We learn that the tribe of Armin were domiciled chiefly in the adjoining county of Lincoln. In King James's time, Sir William Armine sat in Parliament for Boston, Lincolnshire, across the Fens and the Wash from the ancient Fenland port of King's Lynn. Carrying our present search to King's Lynn, my friend the Rev. N. D. Fourdrinier kindly combed the registers of the ancient St. Margaret's Church there, but no entry of Robert's baptism was to be found. Two entries which he obtained from the published *Calendar of the Freemen of Lynn*,[1] however, throw some light: 'John Armyn, tailor, took up his freedom by purchase in 1561–62,' and 'Symon Barnard, fletcher, apprenticed to John Armyn deceased, took up his freedom by apprenticeship in 1565–66.' To these points, through the kindness of Miss Farrow, Mr. Fourdrinier has been able to add an abstract of the will of Margaret Armyn, of King's Lynn, widow (who seems to have been our Robert's grandmother), dated 9 January 1563 and proved in the Archdeacon's Court 13 December 1565, making her son John Ayrmyn (?Robert's father) her heir and executor. From the foregoing details, and from other evidence to be produced later in this chapter, we may construct a tentative and partial pedigree of the family, as shown on the opposite page.

To return now to London records, Miss Denkinger further obtained from the registers of St. Botolph extra

---

[1] Norfolk and Norwich Arch. Soc. (1913), 103, 106.

Aldgate, with christening or burial entries for three of Robert Armin's children,[1] the entry of his own burial as well, November 30, 1615, describing him as 'Free of the Goldsmiths [Company] and a Player.' Had Armin lived the few months longer needed to survive Shakespeare, we should surely have found him in the poet's will, receiving a legacy from his old friend along with his fellow-actors Burbage, Heminges, and Cundall.

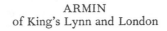

ARMIN
of King's Lynn and London

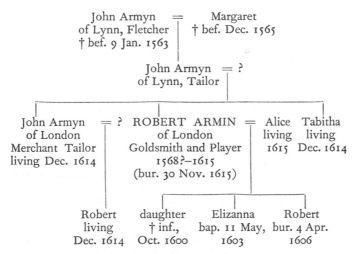

John Armyn = Margaret
of Lynn, Fletcher   † bef. Dec. 1565
† bef. 9 Jan. 1563

John Armyn = ?
of Lynn, Tailor

John Armyn = ?   ROBERT ARMIN = Alice   Tabitha
of London   of London   living   living
Merchant Tailor   Goldsmith and Player   1615   Dec. 1614
living Dec. 1614   1568?–1615
(bur. 30 Nov. 1615)

Robert   daughter   Elizanna   Robert
living   † inf.,   bap. 11 May,   bur. 4 Apr.
Dec. 1614   Oct. 1600   1603   1606

To the above I can now add something more by the discovery at Somerset House of Armin's original will,

---

[1] Bur. 1600, October. 'A woman Chyld daughter to Robart Armin a player of Enterludes the Eleventhe.'

Bapt. 1603, May. 'Elizanna Armin daughter two Robert Armin player the Eleventhe' [named for the two Queens].

Bur. 1606, April. 'Robart Armin sonne to Robart Armin a player of Enterludes the fowerthe.'

dated December 5, 1614, written on two sheets of paper, each signed 'Robart Armyn.'[1] On first reading the long

---

[1] 'In the name of God Amen; the Fifte Daie of December Anno Domini (1614) And in the yeares of the Raigne of oure Soveraigne Lorde James by the grace of god kinge of Englande Scotlande Fraunce and Irelande Defender of the faithe &c, (That is to saye) of Englande Fraunce and Irelande the Twelveth, And of Scotlande the Eighte and Forteth; I Roberte Armyn Cittizen and Goldsmithe of London, the vnprofittable servante of Almightie god, weake in bodie, but stronge in minde, doe willingly and with a Free harte render and give againe into the hands of my Lorde god and glorious Creator, my spirit, which hee of his moste mercifull and Fatherly goodnes gave vnto mee, when hee fashioned mee [in] my Mothers wombe, makeing mee a lyving and a reasonable Creature, nothing doubting but that for his infinite Mercies, sett forthe in the moste pretious bloode of his moste dearely beloved sonne Jesus Christe, oure only Savioure and moste glorious Redeemer, hee will receave my soule into his glorye, and place it in the Company of the heavenly Angells, and blessed saintes, And as concerning my bodie even with a good will and free harte I give it over, commending it to the earthe whereof it came, Nothing doubting but that According to the Article of my faithe, Att the greate Daie of the gennerall resurrection when wee shall all Appeare before the Judgment seate of our blessed Redeemer Jesus Christe, I shall receave the same againe by the Mightie power of God wherewith hee is Able to subdue all thinges to himself, not a Corruptible Mortall, Weake and Vile bodie as nowe it is, But an vncorruptible, immortall, stronge, and perfecte bodie, like vnto the glorious bodye of my Lorde and Savioure Jesus Christe, And as twoching [sic] the Worldlie substance which god of his grace hathe given mee, and made mee Steward of, in this Mortallitie; For the preventing of all controversies and contentions, which many tymes doe arise amongest Deare Freendes for the goodes and possessions of such as leave theire estates vndisposed of, being either prevented by sudden deathe or by protracting of tyme,

[signed] Robart Armyn

vntill such feeblenes and Debillitie of bodie and memorie overtake them, that they cannot sett any certeyne course or order therein, I being as aforesaide weake in bodie but of perfecte memory I hartilie thanke Almightie God for the same, for the prevention of all controversies and contentions as aforesaide which might Arise betweene my lovinge wife and kindered for my saide Worldly substance doe therefore Advisedly and with good deliberation, will and dispose of

108

and devout preamble of this will, one might hastily assume that if Armin dictated such terms to the scrivener he must have been a deeply religious man. But in another

---

my saide Worldly substance as followeth, first I give and bequeathe vnto my brother John Armyne Cittizen and Marchantaylor of London my seale ringe of golde with my Armes on it, Item I give and bequeathe vnto my saide brothers sonne Roberte Armyn a peece of golde or Jacobus of Twentie & two shillinges Item I give and bequeathe vnto my Sister Tabitha my olde Cloake, Item I give and bequeathe vnto Roberte Treate Cittizen and gouldsmithe of London, and to George Blundevell Cittizen and vpholster of London, Eleaven shillinges a peece in remembraunce of love vnto them, Item all the rest of my saide worldly substance whatsoever it be, my debtes being paide and funerall discharged I fully & wholly give and bequeathe vnto my saide loving Wife Alice Armyn whome I doe make & ordeyne my full and sole Executrix of this my last will and Testament, Item I earnestly request and desier the saide Roberte Treate and George Blundevell to bee the supervisors of this my last will and Testament, requesting them Also to Aide and Assist my said Executrix towching this my last will & Testament yf need shall requier, In witnes whereof I have hereunto putt my hande and seale the saide Fifte Daye of December Anno Domini (1614) my saide last will & Testament conteyning two sheetes of paper

[signed] Robart Armyn

in the
hall of
Mr Armyns
howse

Published the Daye and yeare aboue written & the same reade to the Testator by mee John Warnar scrivenor, and the same sealled & subscribed by the said Testator in the presence of [signed] Simon Warren

signum Willelmi W B Brice
and of mee John Warnar London Scr

[Endorsed]

parochie sancti   Probatum fuit hujusmodi testamentum xij die
Bothulphi extra   Decembris Anno domini 1615. coram Magistro
Algate   Willelmo Creke in legibus bacchalaureo Surrogato
                    domini Officialis &c, iuramento prefate Executri-
cis &c, cui &c de bene &c saluo Jure &c. Exhibitum est Inventarium extendentem ad summam—Clx^{li} xiij^s ij^d

(P.P.R. Archd. Lond. A similar entry of probate in Acts, Vol. 5, p. 58.)

will[1] drawn by the same notary, John Warnar, I find this same form repeated almost word for word. What is more, when the said Warnar drafted his own will[2] we discover that he limited the pious preamble to a few words. It is tempting to suspect Warnar of supplying Armin with a long, eloquent and moving form because it would almost double the amount of his work and presumably his fee. Still, we cannot justifiably assume that the testator did not ask for the long form from a true religious motive.

Now for the bequests in detail. In Armin the goldsmith as in his friend Shakespeare we have a player who could 'give arms' as a gentleman. To his brother John—who had also come up to London, and followed their father's trade as a tailor in the metropolis—the trade which finds a place in the title of Armin's verse-translation called *The Italian Taylor and his Boy*—he leaves his treasured gold seal ring with his arms on it; and to his nephew and namesake a gold Jacobus of 22 shillings, both considerable gifts. His sister Tabitha (whose name he had used for one of the heroines of his *Two Maids of More-clacke*) is to have his old cloak. Two friends, the fellow-goldsmith Robert Treate and the upholster George Blundevell, are appointed overseers of the will, with a love-token of eleven shillings apiece. Probably no children had survived, since none is mentioned. His loving wife Alice Armin he makes executrix and residuary legatee.

When the will was drafted, on December 5, 1614,

---

[1] George Axton's, the merchant tailor who was Shakespeare's near neighbour in Bishopsgate: D. & C. St. Paul's, Bk. D, 111 (1614).
[2] Cons. Lond. Reg. Allen 395 (1640).

almost a year before his burial, Armin was 'weake in bodie.' Let us hope that this does not mean a fatal illness lasting close on to a year. His widow took probate of the will some two weeks after the funeral. Though we cannot be sure that the actor suffered no lingering death, it is now clear—contrary to the assumption of J. P. Collier—that he certainly did not die in poverty. The scrivener got a good fee, and refers to him as 'Mr Armin.' He had a house with a 'hall' where the will was drawn, and the inventory of his moveables amounted to the considerable sum of £160 13s. 2d., as much as the contemporary inventories of citizens regarded as fairly well off.

Have we any clue as to Armin's personal appearance? I believe that in *Twelfth Night* a speech of Feste's—his confidential monologue to the audience while disguising himself in the clergyman's gown—reveals something of it: 'I am not tall enough to become the function [of preacher] well, nor lean enough to be thought a good student.' We may conclude that Armin the player was but of middling stature, and not thin! But then Feste goes on, 'but to be said an honest man and a good house-keeper goes as fairly as to say a careful man and a great scholar.' From the mouth of the truant Feste, taxed by his lady with growing 'dishonest,' this is delicious irony. But since in real life the actor Armin was well known to be 'an honest man and a good housekeeper,' we may if we choose also allow Shakespeare and Armin this as a deft stroke in defence of the respectable members of their much-attacked profession.

There is always more in every facet of Elizabethan life than meets the modern eye. For one thing, there was far more in a *name* than there is today. A familiar example of this is their punning heraldry. Every time we look at Shakespeare's coat of arms, the Elizabethans remind us of the literal meaning of his name. Similarly with Armin. Like all the armigerous Armins, the player on his heraldic shield undoubtedly bore *Ermine*, pronounced 'armin.'[1] In contemporary folklore the ermine was believed to prefer death to being stained. Its noble snow-white fur, artificially dotted with black spots to set it off, besides being of Queen Elizabeth's personal colours white and black, was a symbol of purity, truth, and honesty:

> O that honesty,
> That ermine honesty, unspotted ever,
> That perfect goodnesse.[2]

With these associations in mind, we can understand the double appropriateness of the words I have italicized in John Davies of Hereford's hearty encomium[3] on this beloved player, in 1610, while he was still active, and noted like Shakespeare for honesty of life:

> *Armine*, what shall I say of thee, but this—
> Thou art a fool and knave? Both? Fie, I miss;
> And wrong thee much, sith thou indeed art neither,
> Although in show thou playest both together.
> *Honest* Robin, thou with harmless mirth
> Doth please the world; and so amongst the earth
> That others but possess with care that stings,
> So makest thy life more happy far than kings;
> And so much more our love should thee embrace,
> Sith thou still livest with some that die to grace,
> And yet art *honest*, in despite of lets,
> Which earns more praise than forcéd *goodness* gets.

---

[1] Compare the Spanish '*Armin*, the fur of Ermines' (Percivale-Minsheu), and the Italian '*Arminii*, Ermine . . . in armorie' (Florio).
[2] Fletcher, *Monsieur Thomas*, 4.1.   [3] *The Scourge of Folly.*

So play thy part, be *honest* still with mirth;
Then when th'art in the tiring-house of earth,
Thou being his servant whom all kings do serve,
Mayest for thy part well-played like praise deserve;
For in that tiring-house when either be,
Y'are one man's men, and equal in degree;
So thou in sport the happiest men dost school
To do as thou dost—wisely play the fool.

'Some that die to grace' implies that some of the acting 'quality' were noted raffish fellows, no better than they should be. But Armin's ermine-honesty was clearly unspotted by his association with them. And after death Kings and Players will be equal: common Christian servants of God, or 'one man's men.' The love that breathes from these lines is the affection ever inspired by the sound-hearted comedian with the rare gift of spreading happiness.

Two final words about the significance of Armin's name. If we 'hunt the whiter ermine' in Lyly's *Mother Bombie*, we come upon Livia choosing for her samplar 'Among beasts, the foxe and the Ermin, [the ermine] for beautie [and pure truth] and [the fox for wily] policie.' This contrast, familiar to the Elizabethans, may enrich our understanding of what Armin as Feste tells Malvolio: 'Sir Toby will be sworn that I [in my pure ermine-Armin honesty] am no fox; but he will not pass his word for twopence that you are no fool.'

So much for Armin's name. Now let us take a moment to run down his puzzling nickname 'poor Pink'—which he reveals in the course of a letter of 1604 to Lady Mary Chandos. As for the 'poor' part of this, we recall that in Dutch and German the poor are 'Armen' and in canting

English a beggar is an 'Armine': enough to show why the punster Armin (who was not impecunious) could call himself 'poor.' As for 'Pink,' we find illustration of the probable source of this nickname in the 1580 accounts of Queen Elizabeth's Great Wardrobe:

> 'for mendinge the furre of our Robe kertle & circoate of purple veluet with ten tymber [i.e. 400 skins] of Army- ons, fower thowsand pouderinges and fower thowsand pinkes . . .' [1]

A *pink* was a small ornamental gash or cut; a modest diminutive for our Armin. Not even a pelt of the little ermine, but a tiny cut in it![2] Not content with one mean- ing only, Armin quipped upon another sense of *pink*, in still more modestly styling himself 'Snuff, Clown of the Curtain Theatre' (*Clonnico de Curtanio Snuffe*), meaning 'a miserable flickering candle-end of wit' that needs to be *'pinked'* or *snuffed* to maintain its feeble flame. For illus- tration we have Nicholas Breton's *The Good and the Bad*, with 'he is but the snuff of a candle, that *pink* it ever so long it will out at last'; also Lyly's *Pappe with an Hatchet*, 'olde Martin with a wit worn into the socket, twinkling and *pinking* like the snuffe of a candle.'

To turn for information from Armin's name and sobriquets to the craft he had mastered in addition to his actor's art is to find ourselves no less rewarded. As a goldsmith, the typical tool of his trade was naturally the touchstone, defined by the *Oxford English Dictionary* as a smooth piece 'of black quartz or jasper, used for testing the quality of gold and silver alloys by the colour of the

---

[1] P.R.O., L.C. 5/35/223.

[2] 'Mouscheter . . . *to pink, or cut with small cuts*' (Cotgrave- Howell). 'Tagliuzzi, *little cuts, gashes; . . . Also small pinkes in clothes*' (Florio, 1611).

streak produced by rubbing them upon it.' And for use with the touchstone the goldsmith kept at hand his sheaf of proof-needles of graduated colours: small strips of gold or silver of a known or standard fineness, for comparison and matching with the streak of metal-colour made on the touchstone by the 'touch.' We find as the heraldic crest of the Goldsmiths' Company 'a demy woman clothed, holding in one hand a touchstone sable [black],' and recall that the goldsmith in *Eastward Ho* is suitably named Touchstone.

Elizabethan familiarity with this goldsmith's instrument appears by the frequency of its figurative use in the speech of the day; as for example, 'Reason, the Touch-stone to dijudicate what is good from what is ill' and 'Speech . . . is without question a Touch-stone, discovering as well wise men as fooles.' It was a favourite also for book-titles, such as *The Touchstone of Complexions, The Political Touchstone, A Touchstone for the Time Present, The Touchstone of the Reformed Gospel, The Touchstone of Wit.* 'Touch,' the shorter form of the word, was also common. Witness Shakespeare's use of it in *Richard III*: 'Now do I play the touch, to try if thou be current gold indeed.'

The witty fool is in truth the best index to the quality of other characters, whether in a play or in real life. There is every reason therefore why our goldsmith-playwright Robert Armin created for himself the role of the fool Tutch in his comedy. He held by right to the doubly appropriate name which Shakespeare had given him as the inimitable 'indicator,' Touchstone, in *As You Like It.* Small wonder that the testing-instrument of stone loomed large in Armin's thoughts, and that in his comedy he wrote such lines for himself as 'give a ducket, looke you tucke [touch] it.' 'now am I tri'd on mine own tutch, I am true mettall one way, but counterfeit an other,' and 'Ile fit ye sir, tis here, I am tutch right, hic & ubique, everywhere.' We notice by the way that Tutch's motto '*hic et ubique*, everywhere' is in the tradition of the knavish fool or Vice of the old comedy, as Ben Jonson's character Iniquity shows in *The Divell is an Asse*:

What is he, calls upon me, and would seeme to lacke a *Vice?*
Ere his words be halfe spoken, I am with him in a trice;
Here, there, and every where, as the Cat is with the mice;
True *vetus Iniquitas* [old Iniquity].

And Hamlet with this same *hic et ubique* is jestingly recalling the old Vice when he calls the ubiquitous Ghost 'boy,' 'this fellow,' 'old mole,' and 'truepenny.' Like 'true Roger' or 'trusty Roger', *truepenny* is used in irony. Littleton's Latin Dictionary defines it as *veterator vafer*, 'old crafty knave.' The bad penny is always turning up.

To return to Armin the goldsmith. As an apprentice, he must have found himself at the very centre of England's dealings with standards of gold and silver. For as we have seen he served John Lonyson, and Lonyson was Queen Elizabeth's Master Worker of her monies at the royal mint in the Tower of London. Historians remind us that not the least triumph of Elizabeth's resolute and wise statesmanship was her restoration of the English coinage, debased by her reckless father. One of the most responsible duties of her Privy Council was therefore the 'trial of the pyx': that is, in the presence of the Warden and the Master Worker of the Mint, to 'view the assay,' or oversee the testing and weighing of current coinage in comparison with the standards. This test, England's 'touch' *par excellence*, took place in the Star Chamber of the old Palace of Westminster, to which the pyx or box of standard monies was fetched from the Chapel of the Pyx (the royal treasury within the cloister of Westminster Abbey). Some ancient chests and boxes from the Chapel of the Pyx are still preserved in the Museum of the Public Record Office.

So thorny was this business of the standard of coinage and of 'keeping the touch,' that we find that the decade of Armin's master Lonyson as Elizabeth's chief moneyer witnessed an epic and resounding controversy between him and the administrator or Warden, Richard Martin. Voluminous records of it remain. At the bottom of the quarrel must have lain Warden Martin's desire to get Master Lonyson's job for himself; for immediately upon Lonyson's death in 1582 we see Martin with a warrant from the Council ordering Widow Lonyson to hand over to him the Mint-Master's tools, and carrying on the Queen's coinage thereafter himself. Young Armin, recently apprenticed in the house, doubtless saw the implements surrendered; but we have yet to learn under what goldsmith he finished his apprentice years and was 'made free' of the Goldsmiths' Company. At the Mint he would have been familiar with the sweltering workmen whom Sir Philip Sidney called the 'forswat melters'; and passages in Armin's play recall the hot work at the refining furnace:

> ... is the fire fire
> whose scorching heate dissolves relenting mettall
> Whenas it tries the substance?

> ... images of molten mettall,
> which to drosse dissolvd, appeare as nothing.

               . . . let it come bright fire,
To trie the substance of my loves resolve.

While treating of his play we are led to wonder how the
East Anglian Armin came to lay one of its scenes far away
in the Isles of Scilly, the outposts of Britain aloof in the
Western Ocean. Those undrowned rocky hilltops beaten
by the great blue Atlantic seas stood in strong contrast
to his memories of the flats of the Fenland Wash on the
other side of England, but he describes the glittering sands
of a Scilly island beach as if he had seen them. The
Scillies—the ancients' *Cassiterides* or Isles of Tin—lie off
the tip of tin-producing Cornwall. It would seem that
mere pleasure, and not business, would take a goldsmith,
who was neither a pewterer nor a gunfounder, into the
western realm of the Stannaries. At all events, the thought
of the sparkling beach wakes the jeweller-goldsmith as
well as the poet in him, and we find the hero of his play—
about to make a grave for his lovely Mary (falsely
supposed dead)—exclaiming,

> Dig ho, this golden beach, whose glittering sands
> Shewes with the sunne as Dyamonds set in gold,
> Fitly intombs a jewell of much worth,
> Whose living beauty stains all lapidary.

This passage points us to the other side of Armin's
training, the goldsmith as lapidary. To stroll along the
fifty-five signs of the world-renowned Goldsmiths' Row
in West Cheap would be to see treasures second only to
the Crown Jewels. (Shakespeare's later associate Francis
Langley had sold five tenements in this Row to buy the
manor of Paris Garden, and build the Swan Playhouse.)
Assailed by the sparkling and seductive display, the Eliza-

bethan loiterer might well utter a pun with his sigh, 'The gravers of the golden shows With jewels do *beset* me.' No doubt it was Armin's expertise in gems, their qualities and setting, that led him to select the tale he translated in verse as *The Italian Taylor and his Boy*, from Straparola's *Notti Piacevoli*, giving interesting evidence that Armin, like Shakespeare, was familiar with Italian literature. For example, in one passage of the tale, magic art transforms the Boy into a rare, invaluable Ruby mounted in a ring, against a foil in a gold collet:

> *And in his foyle so lovely set*
> *Faire collited in Gold,*
> *He shinde amongst the Pibbles wet*
> *Most lovely to behold :*
> *So beautifull and sanguine red*
> *The price no value had.*

And the heroine thus defends the Boy-Ruby Ring, in speaking against the wicked disguised magician—showing that a proper understanding of the virtues of gems and of how and why they should be worn was a mark of education and culture:

> *Promise me yet before the King,*
> *As you are what you seeme,*
> *Not for to wrong this Rubie Ring,*
> *But hold it in esteeme :*
> *For many such as you (I know)*
> *Like Æsop's Cocke, i'th dust,*
> *Had rather have a Corne to owe,*
> *Then Stone of such a trust :*
> *You'le weare it in some abject sort,*
> *Or change the propertie,*
> *To make your idle judgement sport,*
> *Not like a Lapidarie.*

We notice now with pleasure that Shakespeare, in writing the part of Feste for Armin, did not fail to give the goldsmith-comedian scope to display his skill in the properties, virtues, and connotations of precious stones. Catching for 'quaint quirks' at the words of the love-melancholic and unstaid Duke Orsino, Feste implores the wise and melancholy Saturn[1] to have a care of Orsino's wits—'Now the melancholy God protect thee' —adding, 'for thy minde is a very Opall.' Thus he deftly implies not only change and variation, but love itself: the opal is Venus's stone. And later in *Twelfth Night*, when we have the Fool dissembling himself as 'Sir Topas the curate, who comes to visit Malvolio the lunatic,' it is clear (as H. H. Furness, Jr. suggested) that the parson's name takes its source not, as some have thought, in Chaucerian reminiscence, but in that virtuous gem, the Topaz. Francis Bacon called it the 'Gold-Stone' or the 'Yellow Topaze,' which, as every Elizabethan knew, was effective against the passion lunatic. Fully to relish the peculiar aptness of Sir Topas's name to the conspirators' therapeutic treatment of Malvolio's case, we should however assist our modern minds with some handbook of contemporary lore on the efficacy of wearing jewels—such as Cleandro Arnobio's little *Tesoro delle Gioie*, 1602. Here in translation is the gist of Arnobio's third chapter, '*del Topazzo*':

Bede, Arnoldus, and Aristotle all hold that the Topaz has great and manifold virtues. It is good against frenzy, ire, melancholy, and such lunatic

---

[1] 'Women are cruel this year, Saturn reigns with strong influence.'—Letter of Thomas Barrington, Apr. 1632. *H.M.C.* 7th *Rep. App.* 548.

passions as be roused up by the demons. Albertus Magnus concurs in its power against the lunatic passions. Camillus Leonardus declares that it drives out lust—*scacci a la lussuria*—and heals the frantic and the mad. The author of the *Hortus Sanitatis* testifies that it abates the heat of lust; and Dionysius Carthusianus, that the Topaz counteracts the lunatic passions, bridles the unchaste stirrings of the flesh, and relieves frenzy.

Accordingly, we see our ecclesiastical Topaz at once go into action with a frontal assault upon the demon of lust, Asmodeus—not only diabolical but even 'hyperbolical'— who has evidently entered into this wretch Malvolio, stirring him to desire Lady Olivia: 'Out, hyperbolical fiend! How vexest thou this man! Talkest thou nothing but of ladies? . . . Fie, thou dishonest Satan! I call thee by the most modest terms.' [1]

Turning his searchlight on the benighted surroundings of the gloomy prisoner, our lustrous and learned Topaz (is he not 'a yellow stone shining very cleare in the darke'?) declares, 'Madman, thou errest. I say there is no *darkness* but ignorance.' His further expert handling of the 'lunatic' wins Sir Toby's delighted applause: 'My most exquisite Sir Topas!' To which the versatile goldsmith-and-gem Armin-Topaz carelessly rejoins, 'Nay, I am for all waters,'—as who should say, 'Topaz? Topaz is simple for an artist like me. Tush, I will do you a beryl, a pearl, a diamond: a jewel of the first water, or of any

---

[1] We remember that Mistress Page's epithet for Falstaff's lewdness in *The Merry Wives* is similarly modest: 'Hang him, dishonest rascal!' And in *Henry V*, so is the Archbishop's, in mentioning certain women's 'dishonest manners.'

water.'[1] Shakespeare's skilful Armin could expertly choose and set for you any stone—on the stage, or in a finger-ring.

Feste's wit is a joy; but Shakespeare had devised a more richly human role for Armin to play in Touchstone, whose bland morosophy or wise fooling is that of a character 'in the round,' and one which also infallibly reveals the true quality of the others. In no case is this revelation made more striking than with Jaques, the other so-called 'original' figure in *As You Like It*. To begin with, it is plain enough that Jaques has neither the stature of a moralist, a cynic, nor yet of an Elizabethan 'malcontent.'[2] To the contemporary ear, his name sounded sufficiently like 'Jacks' to carry connotations of contempt: 'such Jacks,' 'braggarts, Jacks,' 'sly, insinuating Jacks.' And though the name often scans as a dissyllable—Jakŭs—, the second syllable was so light as to permit the play on *jakes* (privy), a term which in the *Lear* Quarto is written *jaques*. We must remember that in Elizabethan pronunciation *waxe–makes* was a good rime: and the contemporary pun on *Ajax* and *A Jakes* should warn us against diphthonging the *a* of *jakes* as in our modern pronunciation of *takes* (tẽⁱks, *O.E.D.*).

So much for Jaques's name; now for his nature. Too inconstant to qualify as 'a snappish finde-fault with all men,' 'a selfe-weening fellow,' or as 'a mar-all, a spoile-all, a busie-headed fellow,' Jaques is not without a per-

---

[1] Suggested in 1785 by Monck Mason. Compare Ben Jonson's Guilt-head in *The Divell is an Asse* on stones: 'o' the right black-water, And very deepe. . . . Here's one o' the yellow-water, I'll sell cheape.'

[2] See O. J. Campbell in *Huntington Library Bulletin*, October 1935.

ceptible taint or smack of each of these worthies. In him we recognize that familiar negation of character, the vain and shallow discontent. He would much rather grow ostentatiously maudlin over a stricken deer, and call the huntsman Duke a tyrant, than discommode himself in helping to get necessary venison. Like the Walrus, however, his sobs and tears in no wise hinder him from devouring his share of the victims. He best resembles a pair of candle-snuffers: 'snibs filth in other men, and retains it in himself.' Quite unprincipled in his own life, he demands the privilege of cheap general satire and railing; vows he envies the licensed fool Touchstone, and loudly longs for a motley coat. Pure sham. It is clear he is not man enough to accept the danger of the whip which the fool's privilege carries with it.

In his encounters with the admirable characters he is inevitably worsted. Not only is his wit easily overmatched by that of Orlando and of Rosalind, but the latter classes him with 'abominable fellows,' and dismisses him for a dullard. Experience, that proverbial mistress of fools, has obviously taught him no more than the tiresome trick of putting on an artificial melancholy. Rosalind sees the far-travelled and empty Jaques as a modern instance of the old saw,

The fool that far is sent, some wisdom to attain,
Returns an idiot as he went, and brings the fool again.

When he pokes his nose into Orlando's affairs, adding an invitation to join in his favourite pastime of railing against the world, Orlando's contempt sums him up as 'a fool or a cipher.'

For lack of better amusement in the forest, Duke

Senior's 'loving lords' usually give Jaques liberty to vocalize his artificial and commonplace mood. Characteristically, he parades it as 'a melancholy of mine own,' insisting that his repeated rumination raps him 'in a most humorous sadness.' But his complete lack of humour betrays itself both in his inability to see himself and in his 'extremity' of laughing at Touchstone. Shakespeare nowhere better exposes the shallowness of Jaques's 'observation' of mankind than when he brings Orlando on the scene desperate with famine but refusing to touch food until he has succoured the aged Adam in his extremity. Here the Christian Duke, who with his fellows in the wild forest endures shrewd days and nights, cannot but be moved by Orlando's great soul and selfless human kindness; and he tries to stir Jaques to sympathy:

Thou seest we are not all alone unhappy.
This wide and universal theatre
Presents more woful pageants than the scene
Wherein we play in.

This thought is inevitably thrown away on Jaques, to whom the sight of another's heroism in misery means nothing. All it elicits from him is the superficial caricature and shallow puppetry of 'All the world's a stage.' For him, the schoolboy is no more than a whining laggard, the lover a furnace on legs, the soldier a suicide for a bubble. Having thus plainly ticketed this 'strange eventful history' as the whimsy of a callous 'fool or cipher,' a 'libertine' whose satisfaction is railing, Shakespeare could hardly have expected posterity to prove so unthinking as to lift this trifle from its context for display as 'Shakespeare's Seven Ages of Man.' Yet Jaques is useful to his author in keeping the feet of this Arcadian comedy on the ground. His shallowness reminds us that not all men are as admirable as the Duke and Orlando, while the capricious gloom he nurses—what the Germans call *der moralisch Katzenjammer*—is an excellent foil to the sincere pathos of the play. But to leave no doubt that the characteristic aura of this 'Monsieur Melancholy' recalls the unsavoury 'melancholy of Moorditch' or that of Haryngton's unmetamorphosed jakes, Touchstone greets the unavoidable Jaques (with a fine touch of modesty) as 'good Master What-ye-call 't.'

The lesser men in the play are diverted by Jaques, but the earnest Duke takes him up too often for his comfort. He therefore learns to avoid the Duke's company, but vents his malicious mockery in doggerel on that noble soul whose sweetness in adversity makes the carper seem ugly:

If it do come to pass that any man turn ass,
Leaving his wealth and ease A stubborn will to please,
Ducdame, ducdame, ducdame,
Here shall he see gross fools as he,
An if he will come to me.

As C. M. Ingleby correctly pointed out, *Ducdame* or *Duc' da mè* is the Italian for 'Duke by myself' or 'Duke-without-a-dukedom.' To this elucidation we may add the reminder that 'Duke' (*Duc* and *Duco* in French and Italian) was a contemporary English name for the great horn-owl or eagle-owl. This *gran duc*, according to Cotgrave, 'is bigger than a Goose, and keeps alwaies in forrests and desart places.' It looks very much as though Jaques in his triple call of '*Ducdame*' is also slyly taunting the absent Duke Senior, the foolish 'Duke-by-myself,' with the 'Duke' or horn-owl, who 'is bigger than a Goose, and keeps always in forests and desert places' such as Arden. Jaques rubs in his satire further by explaining *Ducdame* as 'a Greek [i.e. sly, crafty] invocation to call fools into a circle.' And as a parting shot, he says he will 'rail against all the first-born of Egypt.' The *first-born* is of course the exiled 'ass,' Duke-Senior-without-a-dukedom, who has craftily charmed these grossly foolish friends of his into sharing the miserable gypsy (Egyptian) existence of his exile. Both stanzas, '*Who doth ambition shun*'—the Duke's cheerful acceptance of misfortune—and Jaques's sour parody, are written in the one metre. But the first is chorused out in song, while '*Ducdame*' remains a carper's croak.

To produce the comedy's requisite happy ending, Shakespeare subjects Jaques to the miraculous reformation of character which the fratricidal Oliver and the wicked usurper Frederick must also undergo. It is a novel and docile Jaques who announces that he will visit the suddenly converted Frederick in monkish cell, to learn much matter he was incapable of learning before; an unheard-of Jaques to whom (under the duress of the happy ending) Shakespeare allows the first and only manly speeches he ever utters. This last-minute transformed character is necessarily the reverse of Jaques's true nature, which has been only too evident from the start. Though the essentially vain Jaques must consistently pretend a satirical condescension to the motley fool Touchstone, he finds himself diminished and at the same time irresistibly fascinated by a wit so much more quick, resourceful, and human than his own. His praise of Touchstone's inimitable 'Seven Degrees of the Lie' must be qualified by a surprised 'and yet a fool!' To dress his poor rags of superiority, he calls Touchstone's brain 'dry,' his knowledge 'ill-inhabited' in the body of a professional jester, and gives him the equivocal title of 'a *material* fool,' which, as well as 'substantial,' also meant 'dull' or 'shallow-witted.'[1]

His every contact with Armin the goldsmith as Touchstone however only shows up the poor quality of the metal of Jaques. The usual test which Touchstone applies both to the satire and to the romance and idealism in the play is the age-old one of parody carried with a straight face. Thus, meeting the shallow moralizer Jaques, Touchstone makes his own 'moralizing on the time' shallower still. And for comment on the romantic and 'pastoral' love-making all round him, Touchstone woos Audrey, expecting the worst, and ready to cast her off when time shall serve.

Because his satire leaves no sting, it leaves an effect; and because like Falstaff's it is human, it is winning. In one mood we join with the Christian Duke in accepting the harsh exile in Arden, embracing the sweet uses of adversity; but when Touchstone declares, 'Ay, now am I in Arden, the more fool I! When I was at home I was in a better place,' the appeal to common sense is irresistible. Dowden's view of Touchstone as 'a clown among courtiers, a courtier among clowns' is perhaps too neat. The wit and learning in the role, so characteristic of

---

[1] See Florio: '*Materiale*, materiall, substantiall. Also used for a dull or shallow-witted and grosse fellow, wanting forme.' And Girolamo Bargagli, of the famous Sienese academy of the *Intronati* or 'Thunderstruck,' ironically styled himself *Il Materiale Intronato*, The Thunderstruck Dullard.

Armin, surpass that of any clown. True, in his idiot's robe Touchstone must allow the affectionate Celia to call him 'dullard,' and Rosalind to dub him 'Nature's natural.' Yet though uncannily shrewd, he is no oracle, but a fallible human commentator with a saving sense of humour: 'Nay, I shall ne'er be ware of mine own wit till I break my shins against it.' Aware that 'the wise man knows himself to be a fool,' he yet has his foibles. The worst that could be said of him might be summed in a speech from Lyly's *Mother Bombie* (in which I change the gender of the pronouns), as follows: 'Nay, he is no natural foole; but in this consisteth his simplicitie, that he thinketh him selfe subtile; in this his rudenesse that he imagines he is courtly; in this the overshooting of him selfe, that he overweeneth of him selfe.'

'By all means,' Robin Armin might reply, 'criticize Touchstone, censure me for playing the fool. But when the play is over, *I* have the money you paid to see me act, and *you* are out of pocket. Who's the fool now?' This is no fancy; Armin versified this very point, speaking of himself as 'he':

> True it is, he playes the Foole indeede;
> But in the Play he plays it as he must,
> Yet when the Play is ended, then his speed
> Is better then the pleasure of thy trust:
>> For he shall have what thou that time hast spent,
>> Playing the foole, thy folly to content.

FOOLS IN COLOURS

THOUGH it is absolutely clear that ordinary idiots and the usual domestic jesters were generally robed in the coarse mixed motley, and that Shakespeare and other playwrights, in presenting their fools on the stage made use of this humble dress, it should not be assumed that all Elizabethans limited their jesters' costumes to this prevailing mode. We have not found, indeed, that Queen Elizabeth herself costumed any of her fools and jesters in motley. On the contrary, she made her singular Italian, Monarcho, for instance, still more singular by dressing him in a 'foure quartered Jerken' of red grograin camlet, 'striped downe with blewe vellat layed on with copper gold lace.' Monarcho also enjoyed a remarkable doublet 'of striped sackcloth,' faced with taffeta![1] The preposterous combining of sackcloth with taffeta evidently struck a suitably foolish note, for in the play *Eastward Ho* the character Mildred observes that it is 'like a fool' to 'mix sackcloth with satin.'

Just because the Elizabethan gentry of both sexes showed a rich variety of colour in their costumes, the vain and pretentious betrayed their folly by overdoing a good thing. They put on too many tints, or chose ill-assorted contrasts. In the matter of colour in dress, the dividing line between 'fine' and 'ridiculous' was at least as disputed as it is today. Marston's *Malcontent* found room

---

[1] B.M. MS. Egerton 2806, f. 6ᵛ.

for Bilioso's pointed satire of farmers' sons foolishly setting up as gentlemen: 'They shall go apparell'd thus—in sea-water-green suits, ash-colour cloaks, watchet [light blue] stockings, and popinjay-green feathers. Will not the colours do excellent?' The stock phrase for a ridiculous combination of costume-colours was 'pied' or 'pie-bald.' Originally, of course, 'pied' meant the black-and-white of the magpie:

'Ech day he doth in different colours goe—
Nowe like a *Pye*, all clad in black & white ...'

But the term came to be used in derision of almost any fantastic assortment of colours. George Chapman wrote of 'Pied Vanity, the mint of strange attires,' and of 'the Protean rages of pied-faced fashion.'

Hamlet's word for the foppish and affected Osric, 'this waterfly,' is less usual than the stock nickname 'butterfly,' which was often qualified by 'pied.' In Rowley's *Noble Soldier* certain courtiers are termed 'these pide-winged Butterflies,' and Greene's *Quip for an Upstart Courtier* has two boy-lackeys 'in cloakes like butterflies.' Marston's satire in *The Scourge of Villanie* is similar:

When that 'mong troopes of gaudy Butter-flies
He is but able to jet [strut] it jollily,
In pie-bauld sutes of proud Court bravery ...

Robert Burton averred in the introduction to his *Anatomy of Melancholy* that the original *Chrysalis* was a gaudily-dressed and foolish prince; 'but Jupiter,' says Burton, 'perceiving what he was, a light, phantastic, idle fellow, turned him and his proud followers into butterflies: and so they continue still ... roving about in pied coats.'

Nicholas Breton, in *The Good and the Bad*, likened an

unworthy gentleman to 'a baboon with a pied jerkin.'
And foolish ostentation on the fringes of good society
was betrayed by dressing servants in loud colours: 'a
hired Coachman . . . with a cloak of some pide colour';[1]
'pyed liveries to come trashing after';[2] 'keep your men
gallant at the first, fine pied liveries with gold lace.'[3]
Inevitably, uniforms which seemed to their owners 'fine
pied liveries' struck other observers as 'pied and ridiculous.'

As always, mummers and players turned to extravagance
in colour to catch the eye or to produce a bizarre or
ludicrous effect. Jonson's *Masque of Christmas* presents
a character called 'Mumming,' dressed 'in a masquing pied
suit.' In Breton's contrast entitled *Court and Country*, the
Countryman maintains that 'for apparell, plaine russet is
our wearing, while pied coats among us we account
players or fooles.' Robert Cawdray (*Treasurie of Similes*)
observes that 'children do much wonder and praise those
players which on the scaffold be apparrelled in pied and
peevish garments,' and William Rankins remarks in his
Seven Satires that 'fooles . . . on a pide coat gaze.' Chapman's Clermont (in *The Revenge of Bussy*) agrees that
low comics in startling colours offer very primitive entertainment:

Nay, we must now have nothing brought on stages
But puppetry, and pied ridiculous antics.

And John Taylor in his *Water-Worke* implies the same in
speaking of 'this childish Anticke, doating pie-bald
world.'

[1] John Taylor, *The World Runnes on Wheeles.*
[2] Thomas Middleton, *The Puritaine Widdow*, 4.1.
[3] Jonson, *Every Man Out of his Humour*, 1.1.

The expression 'doting' provides a significant link between the foolish pied coats both of pretentious society and of 'antic' comedians, and the pied coats of those professional fools who did not wear the common mixture called motley. And when Taylor, in *Odcombe's Complaint* —his mock elegy on comical Tom Coryate the traveller— calls up the ghosts of departed professional and stage fools to help him mourn, his imagination fancies them in colours:

> O all you crue, in side pi'd coloured garments,
> Assist me to the height of your preferments.

We can readily collect a small bouquet of references to fools in pied coats. In his 'Character of an Amorist' Patrick Hannay lays it down that the lover's 'imagination is a foole, and it goeth in a pide-coat of red and white.' Webster's Jolenta (in *The Devil's Law-Case*) exclaims,

> 'O my fantastical sorrow! cannot I now
> Be miserable enough, unless I wear
> A pied fool's coat!'

In C. T.'s *Laugh and Lie Down* we find the following passage: 'when this *Mask* had once gone aboute the Roome, comes out a *Foole* in a pied coat, and tells them, they must make an ende quickly, and take their places, for the Lady was comming, to see an Enterlude.' Breton, anatomizing the essence of a fool in his pamphlet *The Good and the Bad*, says that the fool's chief loves are 'a bauble, and a bell, coxcomb, and a pied coat.' And John Davies of Hereford includes in his *Wits Pilgrimage* 'An Epitaph, or what you will, on the death of Maister Meece an harmlesse professed Foole, who shall decease, when it shall please God, and him, made at his earnest request.'

Here he represents Meece employing his pied coat to
make a fool of Death:

> Then, *Meece* sith Death doth play the Foole with thee,
> Showing his Teeth, laughing illfavour'dly,
> Put on his Pate, thy Capp; and on his Back
> Thy pied-Coate put, with ev'rie foolish knack:
> And say (sith hee sittes quite beside the Stoole)
> Looke on the Foole that cannot kill a Foole!

One could add more passages on fools' coats of many
colours, but these extracts are amply sufficient to bring
out the essential point. Such costumes by their nature
were 'antic,' 'vain,' or fantastic, clamouring for attention.
Thus they were the opposite of the 'sad' green motley,
which was common and unobtrusive. The choice of
fools' costume made by Shakespeare and Armin for
Touchstone, Feste, and Lear's Fool was sound. Masters
of the common human touch, they neither needed nor
wished the fantastic. They turned their backs on the
antic show of the pied fools' coats, and took to the
familiar and homely motley.